DHARMA OCEAN SERIES

The Lion's Roar

AN INTRODUCTION TO TANTRA

Chögyam Trungpa

Edited by Sherab Chödzin

Shambhala · Bos

SHAMBHALA PUBLICATIONS, INC.
Horticultural Hall
300 Massachusetts Avenue
Boston, Massachusetts 02115

9 8 7 6 5 4 3 2 1

First Edition

Printed in the United States of America on acid-free paper ∞

Distributed in the United States by Random House, Inc.,
and in Canada by Random House of Canada Ltd

Library of Congress Cataloging-in-Publication Data

Trungpa, Chogyam, 1939–
    The lion's roar: an introduction to tantra / Chögyam Trungpa; edited by
Sherab Chödzin. — 1st ed.
        p.   cm. — (Dharma ocean series)
    Includes index.
    ISBN 0-87773-654-5 (acid-free paper)
    1. Tantric Buddhism—Doctrines.   2. Spiritual life—Tantric
Buddhism.   3. Tantric Buddhism—China—Tibet.   I. Chödzin, Sherab.
II. Title.   III. Series: Trungpa, Chogyam, 1939–   Dharma ocean series.
    BQ8918.T79   1992   91-50365
    294.3'925—dc20   CIP

Frontispiece photo by Michael Scot,
from the Vajradhatu Archives.

DHARMA OCEAN SERIES

In a meeting with Samuel Bercholz, the president of Shambhala Publications, Ven. Chögyam Trungpa expressed his interest in publishing a series of 108 volumes, to be called the Dharma Ocean Series. "Dharma Ocean" is the translation of Chögyam Trungpa's Tibetan teaching name, Chökyi Gyatso. The Dharma Ocean Series consists primarily of edited transcripts of lectures and seminars given by Chögyam Trungpa during his seventeen years of teaching in North America. The goal of the series is to allow readers to encounter this rich array of teachings simply and directly rather than in an overly systematized or condensed form. At its completion, it will serve as the literary archive of the major works of this renowned Tibetan Buddhist teacher.

Series Editor: Judith L. Lief

Contents

Editor's Foreword

The two seminars that make up this book were given by Vidyadhara the Venerable Chögyam Trungpa, Rinpoche, in May 1973
in San Francisco and December 1973 in Boulder, Colorado, re-
spectively. Each bore the title "The Nine Yanas." *Yana* is a Sanskrit
word meaning "vehicle." It refers to a body of doctrine and practical instruction that enables students to advance spiritually on the
path of *buddhadharma.* Nine yanas, arranged as successive levels,
make up the whole path. Teaching nine yanas means giving a total
picture of the spiritual journey.

To give this total picture in 1973 meant a new departure for
the Vidyadhara Trungpa Rinpoche in his teaching in the West. It
meant introducing *tantra,* or *vajrayana,* because the last six of the
nine yanas are tantric yanas. Until the San Francisco seminar,
though students understood that the Vidyadhara's ultimate perspective was tantric, and though he often spoke in general terms
about the tantric approach, specific details were taboo. He turned
aside prying questions about tantra with humor, derision, intimi-
dation, evasion, or whatever other means was handy.

Then he embarked on a new phase in his teaching. In May he
gave the San Francisco seminar, introducing tantra for the first
time as a level of teaching that could actually become available to

his students if they worked through the preceding levels. In the fall he taught the Vajradhatu Seminary, the first in a long series of yearly three-month practice-and-study intensives that took the form of detailed instruction on the nine yanas. The seminaries were not public. Here students who had already received appropriate training were prepared to enter upon tantric practice. Immediately after that first seminary, in December, the Vidyadhara taught the nine yanas to the public again in Boulder, once again holding out the possibilities of the complete path. This time, after each of his own talks, he had one of his students fresh from seminary explain something of what he had understood and experienced there.

Tantra is an astonishing doctrine. It seems to come out of primordial depths of experience and run at all kinds of odd angles to convention and conceptual thinking. It eludes these two would-be stabilizers of human experience; therefore the presentation of it is shocking and raw. One of the slogans that comes out of the tantric Buddhist tradition of Tibet is *tampe tön ni jikpa me,* which the Vidyadhara chose to translate, "The proclamation of truth is fearless." He made that the motto of Vajradhatu, the religious organization he founded, and that motto strongly characterizes the seminars we have before us.

Traditionally the elements of a situation in which the dharma is transmitted are enumerated as the right teacher, teaching, place, time, and students. All five shape the event. The last three factors shaping these two seminars can be evoked most simply by recalling that this was the time in America of hippies and the "spiritual supermarket." It was a period that was a crack between periods. One social minibubble of manners and outlooks had been punctured and let, another had yet to inflate. It was a moment of openness, of exuberance and candor.

Perhaps these elements provide a partial explanation of the extraordinary qualities of the Vidyadhara Trungpa Rinpoche's teaching. In it, there is a near absence of protective reserve.

Guarding and cherishing the essence of tradition, he steps beyond its stone walls to meet his students on open ground. He does not rely on established doctrinal formulations, but speaks from a non-conceptual, essential understanding of things and explains them in terms experiential for his audience. After he has already made an experience clear, he might say, "In fact the traditional metaphor is . . ." or "The traditional term for this is . . ." He sometimes referred to his unique style of displaying the inner heart of the teaching without focusing on its outer details as "finger-painting." This book is an excellent example of how his "finger-painting" can directly communicate insight far beyond the pale of conventional understanding. He does not present us with airtight rehearsals of doctrine. To any audience, then or now, such presentations can become like displays in a glass case in a museum, remote though perhaps fascinating. Instead, here, the complete teachings of buddhadharma are presented fresh and raw, with their odor intact, as personal experience. They are the mighty roaring of a great lion of dharma. Many of those who first heard them are tantric practitioners today.

In this book I have put the Boulder seminar first, because it seemed to provide an easier leg-up for the general reader than the San Francisco one. Chronological purists may want to read them in the other order. I have provided a few explanatory notes for the general reader. Readers with some specialized knowledge can skip them without loss.

> May the sound of the great drum of dharma
> Eliminate the suffering of sentient beings.
> May the dharma be proclaimed
> Through a million kalpas.

Sherab Chödzin
Nova Scotia, 1991

ONE

Nine Yanas Seminar

BOULDER • DECEMBER 1973

I

The Journey

The Buddhist journey is a journey from beginning to end in which the end is also the beginning. This is the journey of the nine yanas, the nine stages that students go through on the path. *Yana* means vehicle or mode of transport. Once you get onto this particular bandwagon, it is an ongoing journey without reverse and without brakes. You have no control over the horse that is pulling this carriage. It is an ongoing process. Beginning this journey is committing yourself to a particular karmic flow, a karmic chain reaction. It is like being born. When you are born, nobody can say, "That was just a rehearsal," and take the whole thing back. Once you are born, you keep on growing up, growing up, getting older, becoming aged, more aged, and then finally you die. When you are born, there is a certain amount of commitment involved—to be born as a human child from a mother's womb, with parents, with a house, and so on.

This journey is a very definite one, absolutely definite, and that is why it is called Buddhism. Although *ism* is a rather ugly suffix, it is a definite "ism." It is a "Buddha-ism," because we are trying to imitate Buddha's journey. And when we try to imitate Buddha's journey, it just so happens that what we are doing becomes an "ism." It is a real journey, and it involves a real commitment. It also involves some kind of dogma. It means associating yourself with a certain doctrine, a certain formulation of truth. We are not embarrassed to call ourselves Buddhists. In fact we take pride in it, because we have found a way, a path, that makes it possible for us to associate ourselves with Buddha, the Awakened One. "Awakened" here means highly awakened, fully awakened, awakened to the point of being entirely sane, to the point where there is no neurosis to confuse our journey. Ours is a completely sane approach. Thus there is room for pride, room for dogma, room for real commitment. That is the quality of the nine-yana journey.

There is a subtle difference between doctrine or dogma or commitment that is based purely on one's own interest in awakening and the same based on defending oneself against somebody else's belief. Buddhism's approach is the former, and in that respect it can be called a path of nonviolence. We are not interested in putting down any other spiritual journeys taking place elsewhere in this universe. We concentrate on the journey we ourselves are taking.

If we were driving on a highway and became fascinated by the oncoming traffic on the other side of the highway, we might become blinded by the glare of headlights coming toward us, lose track of our own steering, and end up in an accident. But we are interested in this one, direct journey. We keep our eyes on the dotted white line that goes with our direction. We might change lanes, of course. There are faster lanes and slower lanes, but we do not try to get on the *other side* of the road. That is unlawful. There are no U-turns allowed.

So the journey is definite, absolutely definite, definite to the point of being dogmatic. It is dogmatic in the sense that there is no room for insanity or confusion.

You might ask, "If there is no room for confusion, since we are all confused, how can we go on this journey? Are you saying that there is no hope for us to travel on this path? Do we have to get rid of our confusion first in order to embark on this journey?" As far as I know, the answer is no, you do not have to get rid of your confusion first. Precisely because of your confusion, because of your bewilderment and the chaos that you experience, this is the most unconfusing journey you can ever take.

If you are utterly confused, you are confused to the point of seeming to yourself to be unconfused. This is what we call "spiritual materialism"—you have your ideas of the good way, the higher path, and so on, and you think you are beyond confusion. [1] In that case, you might try to cross over to the other side of the road, make U-turns. Because you think you are an unconfused person, you presume you have all kinds of leeway. But in our case, since we know we are confused, we stick to our one journey. Since we know we are confused, this becomes the true confusion, which you can walk on—drive along—as the true path. Working on confusion is the basic point. Since we are highly confused, we have a better chance of getting into this kind of direct and real path. Since we are so very confused without a doubt, we have a big chance, tremendous possibilities. The more confused we are, single-mindedly confused, the more we have one direction, one path, one highway.

Sometimes it seems there is an opportunity to interrupt our confusion by taking a break, taking a rest here and there. As you drive along the highway, you see a rest area. How about turning in to that, pulling in for just a few minutes? Or there's a sign, "food, gas, lodging." How about taking a little rest? Those advertisements for a break, those signposts, in Buddhist terms are called the daughters of Mara. They slow your journey. Suppose you stopped for every one of those signposts, you turned off and stopped and then came back to the highway. Your journey would be delayed, would double and triple in length. You wouldn't get to your destination on time at all. You would be delayed. As a matter of fact, you might not only be delayed. You might be seduced into stopping at a particular motel and fall asleep forever. Go the Holiday Inn, celebrate life; go to the Ramada Inn, enjoy the salad bar of the spiritual feast. There are an infinite number of places where you can eat food and fall asleep forever.

What we are saying is we should try to be very practical—get on the highway and don't stop anywhere. Before you begin your journey, fill up your gas tank to the top. Make the journey and don't get tired. If you get tired of driving your vehicle, turn to your friends. Ask them to take the wheel. You become the passenger and *go on*. There's no point in stopping at these places. This is the yana, this is the journey. None of those little seductions of spiritual materialism that are presented to us are worthwhile. Each one of them says to us, "Don't go too far, Stay here with us. Stop at our place. Spend your money here."

In this respect, the Buddhist path is ruthless, absolutely ruthless, almost to the point of being uncompassionate. What we could say is that we are not looking for pleasure. The journey is not particularly geared for finding pleasure; it's not a pleasure trip. It is a visiting trip rather than a pleasure trip. By no means is it a vacation, a holiday. It is a pragmatic journey. You want to see your mother, your father. You undertake the journey to see them, and you keep driving constantly, maintaining your speed. You don't make any of those roadside stops. You just go, you drive straight to your parents' home.

One of the greatest misunderstandings people have is regarding the spiritual journey as a vacation trip with all kinds of nice things happening on the side. It is a direct journey, visiting our relatives. We don't actually want to see them, but at the same time we are intrigued, fascinated by the possibility of seeing them. "I wonder what they're doing. I wonder how they're getting on." That is precisely what our journey is about.

There is a Buddhist term, *dharmata,* which means dharmaness, the isness of reality. Isness is the parents we are trying to visit. This isness might turn out to be chaotic, terribly embarrassing, or maybe fantastically beautiful and enlightening. All the same, we make our journey back home, back home somewhere, wherever it is.

We left our home a long time ago. We dropped out of college, and we've been wandering here and there, hitchhiking. We are leading our life of a hippie or a tripper, or whatever. We've been here, there, and everywhere. Some time ago, we started to think, "I wonder what my mother's doing. Maybe I should phone her and find out." We phoned her, and then we thought, "Now that I've heard her voice on the phone, I'm more intrigued to see her. Maybe I should pay her a visit. Also, maybe my grandmother would be an interesting person to meet again after all these years. Maybe I should go back and pay her a visit. Grandfather, too, maybe I should visit him." That is exactly what our journey is like. Going back to our heritage, our origin, that is the meaning of "journey" here. So it is not a pleasure trip.

A journey like this can be painful. You wonder why you are taking such a journey. It was not long ago that you felt embarrassed by your family. They gave you enormous pain, real pain. There were all kinds of hassles connected with your parents and grandparents. Your memory of them and your memory of yourself in connection with them is painful.

That is the neurosis of our own basic being. It is highly neurotic, completely confused. We carry a fat body or a skinny body, and we have this big dictionary that we carry with us. Each time we open the dictionary we find a word, which is a piece of our subconscious gossip. And each time we find a word, we close down—we get anxious about the whole situation. Then we open this book again and find another word. This produces further anxiety, more subconscious gossip. We're hampered: we're completely crowded, confused, and claustrophobic with all the passion, aggression, and all kinds of other things going on in our minds bouncing back on us.

Sometimes of course, we try to put this off on somebody else—kick somebody or make love to somebody. These involvements provide further fuel for the constantly ongoing fire of our emotions. Even trying to get away from it, to turn our minds toward the higher truths, only adds further fuel. We say, "Now I am getting rid of all that, because I'm getting involved with a higher truth. Whew!" But it comes back again. "Oh-oh," we say, "here I go again." And the same trip goes on again and again and again, constantly. An awareness of unending confusion begins to develop heavily in our state of mind.

We might say, "I'm a happy person. I've got my life worked out. I've found a certain truth that I can rest my mind in. I don't have a problem anymore. My existence is very simple. I've paid my debts materially, psychologically, and spiritually." The more we say and think things like that, the more there is a very subtle but fundamental pin piercing our heart. It says, "Am I doing the right thing? Maybe I'm doing the wrong thing."

An endless journey of this and that, that and this, is going on all the time. We may think that we have encountered a greater truth, the greatest doctrine of all, or we may tell ourselves that we are just beginners—"I'm just a beginner, but I have found a solid point to begin from"—but whatever we think, whatever we tell ourselves, the whole thing is chaos, absolute chaos. We have question after question happening constantly, all the time. We have even lost track of where we're going or of whether we're coming or going. Having heard the truth, we think, "Is that really the truth?" We ask ourselves, "Do I exist or don't I?" Or, "Who am I, what am I?" This kind of experience is not necessarily restricted to LSD trippers, not at all. Even people who are absolutely normal, in the ordinary sense of the term, who think they're doing okay and are on the right track, have the same kind of confusion, a complete mingling and mix-up of this and that, continually woven into each other. It is fantastically confusing, absolutely confusing. We are confused to the extent that we do not even know who we are or what our journey is about.

This is particularly the case with well-known poets, writers, and psychologists. They seemingly work out their trip purely by writing a book or doing a poetry recital or by adopting the role of a teacher and instructing people. That is the only reference point they have. The rest of their mind is completely in turmoil.

The point is, we have to acknowledge this confusion. Let us acknowledge that it is actually there, that it is happening with us all the time. No matter how much we are confused, no matter how chaotic our experience is, we have some reference point that enables us to know that this is happening. There is some little secret corner in us that says, "This is actually happening to me." That is there, even though we do not want to admit our confusion or tell anybody about it. Publicly or privately, we do not want to admit that this is happening, but personally, we know it. It's because of this little secret of ours that we might get offended in the supermarket. The cashier says, "Thank you and take it easy. Take it easy, now." We think, "How could he know? He doesn't really know who I am and what I am. That was just a common phrase he used."

What I'm saying is that though we think our confusion is highly secret, it's actually highly public. In fact the secret is a secret only for us privately; the fact that such a secret is being kept is public. The self-deception is as outrageous as that. Our private parts are common knowledge, whether we believe it or not.

In Buddhist terms, that private-parts kind of pain is known as *duhkha*, which means suffering—the fundamental suffering. So you don't have to ask anybody, not even a teacher or master, what is meant by pain, duhkha, suffering. You just have to refer to things as they are, this thing that we have, our familiar thing that we have. It's this thingy-ness, which seemingly should be kept private and unseen and unknown even to ourselves. But it is public knowledge.

We should admit this infamous, familiar pain. This is the pain that is actually happening. We cannot say that it is just nothing. It is the biggest thing that we have to hide. We plan all kinds of ways to hide it, thinking that nobody will know. It is like the story of the man who was stealing a bell. He covered his own ears so that nobody would hear anything. A lot of people, including those who are supposed to be the smartest, do that. They turn out not to be so smart. We are so very subtle, therefore we end up being so very obvious. It is really very, very embarrassing; and that embarrassment is pain, duhkha, suffering. Trying to hide our private parts does not work out the way we wanted it to.

Realizing this fundamental suffering, the private parts that we stupidly try to hide—being so intelligent and so stupid at the same time—is the first step of the journey, the first step of Buddhism. Buddha taught about this in his first sermon, calling it *duhkha satya*, the truth of suffering. This is the first of the four noble truths. To realize it is a very noble thing, fantastically noble. It is the highest thing you can discover. This most terrible thing that we are trying to hide more than anything has been exposed as the truth, as dharma, as doctrine. The absolute truth we have discovered is that hiding it doesn't work. Discovering that this hidden factor is exposed already is the highest thing of all. It is the real truth, and if we acknowledge it, it is a beautiful truth, a fantastic truth. The hypocrisy of the whole universe, not just of this world but of the whole universe, of this entire cosmic system, has collapsed—by realizing its own hypocrisy. Acknowledgment of our thingy factor as pain is the highest truth, the most powerful weapon of all. It is a fantastic discovery. Once we have acknowledged that, we have no solid ground to stand on anymore. That is the starting point of all the yanas, the foundation.

STUDENT: You seem to advise against resting when you are tired and want to rest. But pushing yourself is spiritual aggression. Where is the medium between those two?

TRUNGPA RINPOCHE: Taking a proper rest is quite different from taking a break from your embarrassment. Usually when we want to take a rest, it means we don't have enough strength to continue our hypocrisy. But taking an ordinary proper rest is quite different from maintaining the showmanship of your hypocrisy. While you are taking a proper rest is the best time to expose your hypocrisy. You can expose your hypocrisy by falling asleep. You can expose yourself simultaneously with whatever else you are doing all the time.

The point is that there is a very abstract feeling that the whole world is my embarrassing private parts and that I don't want to let go of relating to things that way. So I just take a rest so I can maintain my shield, the curtain of my hypocrisy. A person cannot rest in that properly. People work hard even while they sleep maintaining their hypocrisy. A real rest, a real break, comes from letting go of that heavy labor.

STUDENT: So we try to maintain the fiction that we're not suffering, that we're okay?

TRUNGPA RINPOCHE: It's more than that. When you say you're okay, that means you've been able to conceal yourself. Nobody has seen your private parts, therefore you're okay. This is all because you don't want to expose yourself. Real okay would be the result of letting go. That is the meaning of the truth of suffering. It is painful to see yourself letting go and everything being exposed. This is not particularly pleasant. We wouldn't call it blissful, but it is blissful to the extent that it is being truthful. When you realize the indestructibility of the truth, you connect with an entirely different dimension of reality and security. You have nothing to lose, therefore you're okay. This contrasts with the sense of having lots to gain.

STUDENT: Then why does pain and suffering intensify so much as you progress along the path?

TRUNGPA RINPOCHE: Because you are continually realizing that you have further subtle games; you keep uncovering them all the time.

STUDENT: You spoke about going along the highway not looking at the opposite lane, not getting sidetracked. Isn't that a sacrifice of the panoramic awareness you often talk about?

TRUNGPA RINPOCHE: Looking at the opposite lane could hardly be called panoramic awareness. With panoramic awareness, you see the whole scene. There are no sidetracks. Looking at the opposite lane is just one-sided vision, being distracted by one highlight. You lose the rest of the panoramic vision, which can cause an accident.

STUDENT: Does the pride in being a Buddhist that you talked about at the beginning of the lecture have anything to do with the discovery or unmasking of suffering?

TRUNGPA RINPOCHE: That pride is a kind of conviction, a sense of certainty, the sense that you are taking a definite, particular journey, one which does not provide false hospitality or false pleasures, because it's so real. In that perspective, the sense of security is a sense of the groundlessness of security as opposed to a sense of security based on ego's clinging. You have pride in that kind of security, because you begin to have a sense of the looseness of the air you are flying in as you fall to the ground. You begin to realize that the air is a very secure place; the air is what makes it possible that you *can* fall.

STUDENT: Is that the kind of pride that makes the discovery so real?

TRUNGPA RINPOCHE: Definitely, because then you have no trust in anything else besides the fact that you have nothing to lose.

STUDENT: It seems to me that there is far less pain today than there was thousands of years ago when the Buddha taught. Is his teaching that existence is pain still applicable?

TRUNGPA RINPOCHE: We are not talking so much about physical pain but about this thingness in us that creates pain, which is the pain. This is a universal thing, always up to date. Creating happiness in us is beyond technological means. In the midst of trying to create happiness technologically, that sense of thingness will be present all the time. Thus Buddhism is completely up to date, therefore it is dogma, rather than being religion or philosophy. It is like telling a child, "'Those electric burners on your stove may look beautiful, so nice and orangey red, but if you put your finger on them, it will get burned." Buddhism is as simple as that.

S: Is it not the nature of ego that it is always suffering?

TR: The ego suffers even without its expressions, its manifestations. Ego suffers bluntly, itself.

S: It sounds like when you discover suffering as your foundation, it's like building your foundation on sand, or even worse, in the air, like a castle in the air. It leads automatically to a sense of impermanence, to insecurity. It seems strange that that should be the beginning of the path. You have to put up with complete insecurity. The only security you get through discovering truth is insecurity.

TR: Well said. That is what is called in Buddhist terminology *egolessness*. Discovering that is discovering another truth, which is a firm foundation on which you can build the nine stories of the nine yanas, a tremendous castle of enlightenment.

STUDENT: Where does joy come into the path?

TRUNGPA RINPOCHE: Joy can only come when you realize that there's nothing to be joyful about.

S: That sounds morbid.

TR: What do you mean by morbid?

S: It seems to me that joy is as real as pain, and when you feel joy, to say all that there is is pain is to spit in the face of the joy that you feel.

TR: Are you saying that you feel joy when you don't feel pain? Or do you feel pain when you feel joy?

S: Yes.

TR: That's it. Real joy comes when you experience that something is actually there. That is real joy as opposed to something flowery and sweet. The problem of pain is that there is nothing secure; you're about to lose your ground. Usually when we experience joy, it is purely superficial joy with pain going on beneath the whole thing. Real joy comes when you realize the superficiality of that experience. Then you begin to realize that there is something really happening, whether in the form of pain or pleasure. Then you have the real security of a real discovery of truth. That is actually solid. Joy is related with the solid experience of securing one's ground. Real security could be either pain or pleasure—it is that something real is happening. That is why joy is synonymous with truth. From that point of view, the discovery of the first noble truth, the truth of suffering, is the discovery of real fundamental joy. Because suffering is real; it's absolute. There is nothing other than suffering, and it is very solid and fundamental. It is heroic, indestructible, and beautiful.

STUDENT: Can you explain again what you mean by suffering?

TRUNGPA RINPOCHE: The idea of suffering here is the thingness in us, which is very lumpy and slightly inconvenient. It is the awkwardness in us, which is not very nice or pleasant or flowing. There is something that is in the way that doesn't allow us to be free-flowing. There is a vast thing that is in the way somewhere. That's the fundamental suffering. It is not particularly painful in the ordinary sense of physical pain. But it is in the way. It stops us from flowing. In that sense, suffering could be regarded as synonymous with the idea of a "hang-up."

S: It seems that you don't always have to be suffering, though.

TR: Well, you always have a thing with you, whatever you do. You don't have to be suffering all the time, but you have a thing all the time. The thingy-ness is suffering, though it's true you don't have to be experiencing painfulness all the time.

S: Should you just forget about distinguishing between pain and pleasure?

TR: It's not particularly a question of distinguishing pain and pleasure. The only thing that matters is to begin to realize your thingness, your beingness, that fundamental and deep feeling of awkwardness. That seems to be the point. You might experience pain and pleasure as two or as one, or you might feel that either is okay, you don't care. But still there is this thing that says that pain and pleasure are one. This thingness is happening there—as if you swallowed a lump of rock and it's still in your stomach.

S: Is that real?

TR: It's up to you. It's real as far as you are concerned, if you are talking about it. In that sense, of course it's real. The more you discuss it, the more real it gets. In fact, it becomes a belief, a hang-up. It is definitely there.

STUDENT: A moment can be a warming thing and feel good, and it can also be a burning thing—

TRUNGPA RINPOCHE: It doesn't matter. The dichotomy is there.

Ego and pain is a mystical experience, actually, which transcends both pleasure and pain and thingness and thinglessness. But still there is this thing there that is happening. Right there. That could be called spiritual experience, if you like. What I mean by spiritual experience is the indefinable, ineffable experience of thingness. It is beyond words, beyond concepts. But it is definitely there, hanging on there. It is a mystical experience that everybody has.

2

Hopelessness

We have discussed the nature of pain. That leads us to the subject of commitment, or discipline. What is meant by these words is committing ourselves to what is there, which is pain. The discipline is realizing that this commitment is self-existing. There is no way we can get out of this commitment, so we can make it a wholehearted one.

At this point, we have to understand the origin of pain. As we said, there is that sense of thingness that is hanging out with us all the time. It is part of our shadow. It constantly speaks to us the unspoken word of embarrassment, of inconvenient confusion. As we said, this thingness is connected with suffering and pain. Acknowledging that is our starting point.

It is more than just a starting point, because it inspires us to look further. It inspires us to discover what is behind that awareness of thingness. For example, I personally cannot say I love you or I hate you. There is something that holds us back, that is preventing us from saying such things. It is a sense that we do not want to commit ourselves to becoming involved with embarrassing private parts. And that thingness there that is holding us back has a back and a front. It is just a face, a mask. If you examine it, if you look at somebody who has a mask on and look behind it, you find all kinds of strings and knots. You begin to understand how this person keeps his mask on—with all the bundles of knots in back. Exposing this mask is discovering the origin of pain, of suffering.

The unmasking process is connected with the second yana, the *pratyekabuddha* yana. The mask develops when we try to trace our origins, trace back and back to the origin of the origin. The mask develops from our wanting to ignore ourselves as a confused person to begin with. There is a traditional image for this process of ignoring. It is called the blind grandmother.

The blind grandmother was the creator of our whole family, the whole race. She is also a professional in relating to all the functioning of mental games, ideas, objects, and so forth. But at the same time, she's blind. She can't see what's happening right *there*, right *now*.

When we begin to understand the blind-grandmother principle, we realize how our process of ignoring, of not relating to the blind-grandmother-ness, is constantly creating further karmic chain reactions. Further levels of this process develop. The image for the next level is the potter. The potter makes a pot. He spins his potter's wheel around. He throws mud, a dough made of mud, on his wheel, and in accordance with its speed and how he holds his hands, the potter makes a pot. He makes a pot out of the feeling, which is the volitional action of karma.

We have this thingness, this embarrassment, hanging out in our state of being. It is extremely embarrassing and inconvenient. When we look back, we want to ignore this; we don't want to know anything about it. We might say, "It's not me; it has nothing to do with me. It's somebody else's doing. She did it. He did it. I'm clean. I'm in the clear. My only duty is to stick to this thingness." So we expand ourselves based on this thingness. We explore further and further and further. Having created these karmic situations, we go on with all twelve links of the karmic chain of existence, of our basic makeup: ignorance, volitional action, consciousness, name and form, sense perceptions, touch, sensation, desire, grasping, the further grasping that is copulation, birth, old age and death. And we are back to square one. We go through all those processes, and each one has its traditional image.[1]

This entire map has been seen clearly, thoroughly, and completely by Buddha. Because of Buddha's teaching, we know this entire map of our basic psychology and the origin of that thingness of ours in all the twelve causal links of karma. That thingness is created by going around and around through these twelve again and again. There is birth and death, which leads to a further birth, then ignorance and karma again. It is like a whirlpool, continually circling. That is what is called *samsara*. We go around and around and around in a circle. The end is the beginning. Each time we look for the end of the beginning, we create the beginning of the end. Each time we look for the beginning of the end, we create the end of the beginning. Each time we look for the end of the beginning, we create the beginning of the end. We go on and on in this way. We are in samsara, constantly going around and around trying to catch our shadow. The shadow becomes us, and we become the shadow again. It's a constant circling, an endless game. Endless game after endless game after endless game. There are so many games happening.

What we are discussing at this point is the hinayana level, which involves making a complete study of the four noble truths. We are discussing the second noble truth, which is the truth of the origin of suffering. The origin of the suffering of our thingness is circling with speed. The origin of the suffering is the speed. Graspingness, re-creating one karmic situation after another. That is the basic point here.

This is all pretty ironic, maybe even funny. We could laugh at it—there is such foolishness taking place. It is such a foolish thing that we do. Isn't it ironic? Isn't it funny? Isn't it actually absurd? Ha ha! But it is we who are ha-ha, and it turns out to be very grim actually. We might think, "Ha ha," but it is not all that ha-ha, because it is *our* psychological portrait the way Buddha described it, which happens to be highly accurate. It's very scientific. It's very funny.

What's next? Your guess is as good as mine. What's next after what's next after what's next? What's next? Could we get out of this? Trying to get out would be another circle? Sure we could get out of this. We could get out, and then we could get back in, and then we could start all over again.

You are expectant: "Tell us more" [your expressions say]. Sure. By telling you more, we could get into it, then we could get out and get into it and then we could get out and get into it again.

As a matter of fact, the situation is pretty scary, haunting, frightening. In fact there's no ground except the speed itself. No ground, and we go on and on. We could discuss the next subject and give birth to the next thing; then we'd have volitional action, karma, pain and suffering, touch, desire, copulation, death and old age, birth, ignorance all over again. All over again.

"Tell us about freedom, enlightenment." Sure. By all means. But then: all over again. You get out, you get in. You're liberated. You get onto the liberator's bandwagon, and you take a journey, and you come back. You want to be victorious, win a war of some kind: then you go around all over again, all over again.

We are not making fun of the samsaric world, not at all. We are taking the whole thing very seriously. This is a serious matter. It is a life-and-death matter, very serious. We are talking about reality, freedom, enlightenment, buddhahood, if I may be so presumptuous as to use these words. We are talking about something that is actually happening to us. But so far we haven't touched upon the *heart* of the thing at all. So far we have just discussed the nature of our reality, the confusion that goes on in us all the time. "Nothing new," you say. That's true.

Ladies and gentlemen, you are so faithful and so honest and so straight-faced. I appreciate your seriousness and your long faces, listening to me. That's beautiful—in a way. On the other hand, it's rather grotesque seeing you with your long faces trying to find out about enlightenment.

From this chair, I see lots of faces without bodies, serious faces. Some are wearing glasses, some are not wearing glasses. Some have long hair, some have short hair. But in all cases, it's a long face, made out of a skull wall. These faces—if I had a big mirror behind me, you could see yourselves—are so honest, earnest. Every one of you is a true believer. Every bit of even the glasses you are wearing is a true believer. It is very cute and nice and lovable. It's beautiful—I'm not mocking you at all. I appreciate your patience. You had to wait for a long time and it's late, and now there are all kinds of other things. You're hungry. Probably you had planned to eat after the talk. Probably you are not used to sitting on the floor and would like a nice comfortable chair. All kinds of things go into making up that earnestness. But there is one thing that we haven't touched upon yet, which is that the whole thing is completely hopeless.

Hopelessness. There's no hope, absolutely none whatsoever, to be saved. Hopelessness. Let me define the word *hopelessness*.

Hope is a promise. It is a visionary idea of some kind of glory, some kind of victory, something colorful. There are trumpets and flags, declarations of independence, all kinds of things that are hopeful. Nevertheless, we want to find out the truth here. Discussing the twelve *nidanas,* the twelve causal links in the karmic chain reaction that goes on all the time, and all the time, *and* all the time, we see that we have no chance, none whatsoever. As long as we possess a body and our face, our face and our facade, we have no chance at all of being liberated, none whatsoever. It is as hopeless as that. There is no hope, absolutely no hope. We are going to be drawn into, and drowned in, a deep pool of shit, an ocean of shit, that is bubbling, gray in color, but smelly at the same time. We are drowning in that all the time. This is true; and the situation is hopeless, absolutely hopeless.

We might think, "I'm very smart, extraordinarily smart. I've read all the books on Buddhism, about the twelve nidanas and about everything else. I have the answers. I've read about tantra. I've read about Naropa and Milarepa.[2] I've read Meister Eckhart, the medieval mystic who talks about beautiful things. And I've even read about Don Juan, who says wonderful things about the nature of reality.[3] I've read Krishnamurti, who is very sensible. I'm hopeful, obviously. There's *got* to be a way out somewhere. There must be something. Things can't be all that gray and hopeless."

But what authority do we have? We've just read the books. Maybe we have a friend who has also read the books, and we comfort each other: "Hey, did you read that book? Isn't that great?" "Sure. I agree with you." We build up a whole organization of believing each other and we make each other feel good. However, there's no lineage, no authority. There's no transmission of information from somebody else's true experience. We have no idea whether Don Juan exists. Maybe he's purely Carlos Castaneda's trip. For that matter, we also have no idea whether the books *Meditation in Action* or *Cutting Through Spiritual Materialism* were really written by myself. Maybe they're somebody else's idea of how things should be. The whole thing is subject to question. Possibly all the miracles described in *The Life and Teaching of Naropa,* translated by Herbert Guenther, supposedly translated by Guenther, were just made up. Do we really know that there was such a person as Naropa at all? How do we know there was such a person as Meister Eckhart? And is it possible that what he said was not true, even if there was such a person? And we have no idea about the actual origin of the *Bhagavad Gita,* which contains divine instructions concerning warfare. We have no idea.

Sometimes one wonders who is fooling whom.

Who thought of the idea of enlightenment, actually? Who dreamt up God? Who proclaimed himself as god over all the earth? It seems that the whole thing is full of shit, actually, if I may use such language. Full of dung.

Sometimes we ask questions because we are really frustrated

and we hope to get something out of asking them. Sometimes it is because we are feeling slightly relaxed and want to expose any intrigues that may be going on. Maybe some people are playing a game at our expense, and we would like to expose it. Such trips are constantly going on in our minds. But one thing we haven't come up with is a real understanding of those trips. This is because we haven't fundamentally faced ourselves and the notion of hopelessness. All these messages in scriptures, textbooks, information media, magical displays—whatever we have—are not going to help us. They will just reinforce our blind-grandmother principle of complete ignorance, because we haven't given up any hope. We're still looking around to see if somebody's cheating us. We still believe everything might be okay if we could beat that cheating. That is actually our problem. Nobody has given up hope of attaining enlightenment. Nobody has given up hope of getting out of suffering. That is the fundamental spiritual problem that we have.

We should regard ourselves as helpless persons. That is the first spiritual step we can take. Taking this step is entering what is called the path of unification.[4] It is giving up hope; it is the step of hopelessness. The first path, which comes before this, is called the path of accumulation, in which we gather a lot of materials around us. Then comes the second path, the path of unification, which is giving up hope, totally, and at the same time realizing our helplessness. We have been conned by all kinds of trips, all kinds of spiritual suggestions. We've been conned by our own ignorance. We've been conned by the existence of our own egos. But nothing that has been promised is actually happening. The only thing that is going on is karmic volitional action, which perpetuates our desires and our confusion. Relating with that is the second path, the path of unification.

The reason it is called the path of unification is that there is a sense of uniting ourselves with ourselves. There is a path, there is a goal, and there is a practitioner of the path; but we realize that at the same time those are purely stage props, and the situation is utterly hopeless. We have no way of getting out of this misery at all. Once we realize that there's no way of getting out of this misery, we begin to make a relationship with something.

If we end up in prison with a life sentence, we decorate our cells with pinups and graffiti and make ourselves at home. We might begin to have more gentle feelings about the prison guard and start to enjoy the meals that are presented to us in prison.

Our problem all along has been that we have been too smart, too proud. Our feeling is: I want to stick my neck out all the time. I don't want to relate with anybody else; I want to get enlightened. I'm going to be higher than the rest of you. I don't want to have anything to do with you at all.

That kind of attitude has been the cause of slowing down our spiritual journey. We would do better to take the attitude of the prisoner. Once we realize that we are trapped in our twelve ni-danas, imprisoned, we begin to relate much more. We give birth to compassion in our prison cells. And our existence begins to make much more sense based on what we actually are.

I'm afraid this is very, very depressing. Still, it's heroic at the same time. As you acknowledge the basic situation, you become a drummer of the dharma; you fly the flag of the dharma in your prison cell. You understand that your prison cell is made out of walls: this wall, that wall, this wall and that wall. And you have a simple floor and a simple meal. But those things become an interesting monastic situation. It is exactly the same as being in a monastery. Being in prison is the same thing.

That is why this yana is called the pratyekabuddha yana. *Prat-yekabuddha* means "self-enlightened buddha." You care about your environment, which is necessary, important, very basic, and also tremendously fun. The fun of hopelessness is very powerful, fantastic.

I'm afraid this is very boring. You see, Buddhism is the only nontheistic religion. It doesn't contain any promises, or doesn't permit any. It just suggests the basic necessity of working with ourselves, fundamentally, very simply, very ordinarily. It is very sensible. You have no complaint when you get to the other end of the trip of Buddhism. It's a very definite journey.

Perhaps we could have a discussion, if you don't feel too depressed.

STUDENT: From what you were saying about hopelessness, I guess it could help one relate to one's environment better, but there is something else. Maybe I'm thinking of another kind of hopelessness, but it seems that hopelessness takes away the inspiration to practice at all. And the same thing in relation to the teacher. If you see him as not being able to save you either, it takes away your inspiration for relating to the teacher.

TRUNGPA RINPOCHE: What's the problem?

S: That seems to me to contradict what you were saying about hopelessness being a way to make a true relationship with the teaching.

TR: Hopelessness is getting into the teaching more because you have no choice. When we think about hopefulness, that involves choices of all kinds. But when you realize that there's no hope at all, the way we were talking about, you end up with just yourself. Then you can generate teachings or expressions of teachings within yourself.

STUDENT: What influences you to slow down if you find yourself speeding?

TRUNGPA RINPOCHE: Hopelessness, obviously. The more you speed, the more frustrated you get. So there's no point in speeding. It's hopeless.

STUDENT: Could you distinguish between hopelessness and despair?

TRUNGPA RINPOCHE: Despair is still hopeful, and hopelessness is utterly hopeless. There is no ground to hang on to. You are completely wiped out, therefore you might hang on to your basic being.

Despair is a resentful attitude. You are in despair because you have a sense of retaliation against something or other. Hopelessness is a very genuine, beautiful, simple act. You're hopeless—it's a fantastic thing. You really *are* hopeless then, you know. There's no trips about it. It's clean-cut.

STUDENT: Rinpoche, does this mean that a person has to experience a lot of suffering before he becomes really hopeless? Or could it just happen on the spot?

TRUNGPA RINPOCHE: Both.

STUDENT: Rinpoche, it would make no sense to try to give up hope. If you did that, you would be hoping not to hope. How do you give up hope?

TRUNGPA RINPOCHE: You don't. You're stuck with hope. And then you're disgusted with it.

STUDENT: If there's no trick to giving up hope, how do you manage not to shoot yourself?

TRUNGPA RINPOCHE: Shoot yourself?

S: Yes.

TR: I don't see the connection.

S: When you're faced with being a fake, that causes panic for sure.

TR: But shooting yourself is creating more pain.

S: Not for long.

TR: Really? How do you know? If you regard the body as the problem, then obviously you might be able to destroy your body. But the whole point here is that your mind is the problem. And you can't get a gun that will shoot your mind. Let us know if you find such a gun.

STUDENT: It seems you're saying that the only hope is hopelessness.

TRUNGPA RINPOCHE: That's true.

S: But that's a contradiction.

TR: No, the only hope is hopelessness. "Only hope" means that the ground, our sense of security, is the only hope, which is hopeless—you have no ground. You don't make yourself into a target [for the pain] in any way at all, which is hopeless. The only hopelessness is not to provide yourself as a target.

STUDENT: Isn't that true because when you have no hope, there are no expectations? You cease making judgments, so you like whatever you've got?

TRUNGPA RINPOCHE: That could be said.

S: Isn't that the beginning of joy?

TR: Let's not rush too fast.

STUDENT: Hopelessness is: mind and body are equal? If body and mind are both dropped . . . hopelessness doesn't become. So without hope and with hopelessness, would—

TRUNGPA RINPOCHE: Please don't try too many angles. It is hopeless *straight*. You can't get around it. It will bounce back on you.

STUDENT: Is seeking the mind of a pratyekabuddha still in the realm of hope?

TRUNGPA RINPOCHE: What I have been trying to say is that the mind of a pratyekabuddha is hopeless. We have gotten as far as that, the second yana. The first yana is the acknowledgment of pain. The second yana is the pratyekabuddha realizing hopelessness, realizing the hopelessness of the circle of samsara.

STUDENT: Does the experience of hopelessness always have to be painful? It would seem that after a while you couldn't keep up the pain or the pain would change to something else.

TRUNGPA RINPOCHE: In the beginning it's painful, but in the end, it's reality.

STUDENT: Do you have to realize the truth of your own death before you can become hopeless?

TRUNGPA RINPOCHE: No, your own death is also hopeless. They go together. Your death is hopeless.

STUDENT: At one point, you talked about discipline. You said getting at the origin of pain involved discipline. How does that discipline relate with how you get to hopelessness?

TRUNGPA RINPOCHE: Being faithful to your hopelessness is discipline.

3

The Preparation for Tantra

Since our time is too limited to take a slow, extended journey through the nine yanas, we are going to make a jump. We are going to discuss now the preparation for tantra, which is the mahayana path. First we prepare ourselves in such a way that we have a chance to know just ourselves. Then we begin to know otherness, and then we know everything in mandala perspective.[1]

This approach is based on a sense of individuality and on a sense of egolessness at the same time. What happens with the sense of our individuality here is that, in giving up hope, in reaching a state of hopelessness, complete and total hopelessness, a sense of openness begins to develop simultaneously [which contains an element of egolessness]. Because we have given up hope completely, utterly, totally, there is a sense of opening. That particular sense of openness is called faith or devotion. We have completely tired ourselves out, exhausted ourselves beyond our hopefulness. We realize that life is hopeless and that any effort we put in to gain further experience is also hopeless. Then we get into a real understanding of the space between us and our goal. That space is totally and completely full. And that fullness is what is called faith.

Let me give you a Buddhist-dictionary definition, the definition of faith. Faith here means dedication to and conviction in one's own intelligence, which permits one's own intelligence to begin to manifest as one's guru, teacher, spiritual friend. You have trust in the basic truth of what you are, who you are. You have some understanding of that, and therefore there is tremendous trust. Trust in oneself in turn radiates further trust toward the other. In this case, the other is your spiritual friend, guru, your master, your teacher. The other acknowledges your existence, and you acknowledge the other's existence, and that provides a very solid base of security and well-being. There is a sense that finally you are completely and fully taken care of. That is the definition of faith.

Let me go over that to clarify it further. The definition of faith is: you recognize your existence, which is in turn based on somebody else acknowledging your existence at the same time. This is not a matter of blind faith. It is awakened faith, real faith. You have pain, you are hopeless, and you have somebody else who says, "That's you." This validates your hopelessness. As a result of the agreement that happens between you and the other—your spiritual friend or guru—you realize that something constructive is happening.

It is not purely guesswork. There is a sense of faith based on realizing your hopelessness and having that hopelessness acknowledged by your spiritual friend. You feel secure in the absence of security. There is a sense of trust there.

This is the mahayana path we are discussing here.

Then we have a second category after faith, which is called vigor. The Tibetan word for that is *tsöndrü*.[2] Vigor here has the sense of energy. You are not tired of yourself and you are not tired of working with your spiritual friend or the rest of your friends either. Out of the hopelessness comes inspiration, which brings vigor and a sense of joy—after all, there is something out there that is workable. So you have a feeling of inquisitiveness, an interest in rediscovering your hopelessness [from a different angle]. You have faith in your hopelessness and the communicative relationship you have established with your spiritual friend. In other words, you have devotion. And then beyond that, there is a sense of energy. You are intrigued by the whole thing. You feel something highly intriguing: "Maybe after all there is something in this." It is true, maybe there is something happening. Something's cooking. This sense of intrigue or mystery also ignites your energy, your vigor.

This is like a mad archaeologist who finds a spot to dig. He digs faster and faster and faster. He employs more people to help him. He thinks, "Maybe I'm going to discover gold or a tomb, a temple or a hidden city." It's possible. There's actually something taking place. But this doesn't turn out to be so much on the fantasy level. There is something realistic happening.

That's vigor. *Virya* is the Sanskrit word for this. The definition of *virya,* our second Buddhist-dictionary term, can be understood like this: a person becomes highly inspired, therefore highly inquisitive; therefore he does not become tired of his task. He's inspired, intrigued, tickled. That's the definition of *virya, tsöndrü.*

The great Indian teacher Shantideva talks about tsöndrü in his writings.[3] His definition of it is "taking delight in the virtue of rediscovering oneself." There is this sense of delight and inquisitiveness.

The next category, number three, is *trenpa* in Tibetan, which means awareness, intelligent awareness. At this level [the mahayana], one practices the six perfections or transcending actions (Skt. *paramita*), which are generosity, morality, discipline, vigor (energy), patience, meditative awareness, and knowledge. All six of those happen with awareness. In talking about awareness, we don't mean that you have to meditate on a certain thing you've been told to meditate on. It is not a question of sitting down and gazing at a candle in order to try to develop awareness, or sitting listening to the traffic trying to daze yourself with that sound. Awareness here is pragmatic awareness of what is actually taking place in the realm of your consciousness, in the realm of your intelligence connected with your sense of being.

You are what you are. You have sense consciousnesses, six of them according to the Buddhist tradition. The sixth one is mind-consciousness, and the other five are sight, sound, smell, hearing, taste, and touch. The sixth one, mind-consciousness is also regarded as a sense organ—brain and heart work together. And the sense of being takes place there. The awareness that we are talking about here is definitely connected with that sense of being.

As you sit listening to me talk here, you also realize that you are sitting on the floor, which is padded with cushions. The temperature of the room is agreeable. It does not distract your attention. There is no distracting noise to keep you from listening, no traffic sounds, no babies crying. You have a sense of being here, which is also a sense of well-being. You feel well clothed; your clothes are appropriate and suited to the temperature. You can sit here and listen with that sense of well-being, which is awareness. There's an overall awareness of a relaxed state. Things are physically okay, psychologically conducive.

You might feel a bit overstuffed from dinner or somewhat hungry, looking forward to going home and eating. But those discomforts and desires have become relatively distant, and your main fascination and intrigue can function properly here in this room. That is awareness of well-being that is happening to you right now.

If we want to define that for our Buddhist dictionary, we could say that awareness means a person can tune himself in to certain mental objects and also to a sense of being, or well-being, thoroughly and without distraction. The Sanskrit of the Tibetan *trenpa* is *smriti*. Literally it means "recollection." This is not particularly recollection in the sense of going back to the past. It has more to do with renewing one's habitual patterns, habitual patterns that do not require your further attention. You can be as you are in your basic form. There is a sense of relaxation, which is necessary in order to proceed on the bodhisattva path.

The next is number four, meditation; in Tibetan, *samten*. Here meditation is an extension of the sense of well-being, or awareness, that we've been talking about. There is a feeling of understanding and a feeling of security, which enables you to let go of your mind. The definition of meditation here is the ability to be as you are without further contrivances to make yourself comfortable. The definition of meditation is just a sense of being, a sense of isness that is happening.

Here you are listening to me, listening to this particular "broadcast." You are listening to Radio Peking. You are listening to Radio Peking, but suppose you turn off your radio. Then you find yourself suspended somewhere. You were listening, then that radio was turned off that you had become accustomed to listening to, and you are still there listening to the silence.

It's like television watchers late at night, who will watch up till the very little last dot that appears on their screen. They will watch up till the last little thing when the whole thing dissolves. (In England, an announcer tells you not to forget to turn off your set when the broadcast is over—a very domestic touch.) You turn off your set and you're suspended somewhere, still inquisitive and awake and watchful. That is the state of meditation that we are talking about here. Having turned the set off, you're still watching, but watching nothing. You know you have turned off your set, but you are still there, very awake and ready for something. At the same time, you know that you are not going to get into any entertainment anymore. You've had enough of it. That sense of suspension and of vacancy. Meditation in this sense is like that vacant aftereffect of watching television or listening to the radio. The set is *off,* and you are still fully awake and fully there.

Suppose I said now, "This lecture is over. This is the end. I bid you good night." The moment you heard those words, you would have a sense of your antennae beginning to retract into your basic being. "Wow, the whole thing's gone, finished." And you'd have a sense of well-being taking place. That is the meaning of meditation, samten.

The Sanskrit word for this is *dhyana,* which is the equivalent of *zen,* a sense of meditative absorption without anything in your mind at all to grasp on to. Your television set is turned off, your antennae are retracted: no further entertainment. Yet you are there, definitely there.

There is something very ironical, very funny about this. There is some kind of humor involved here. One catches a glimpse of one's own seriousness: "Now I have turned off this set, and I am still here." You are very serious—something very real is taking place. Empty space. There is a sense of beingness that takes place there that is the essence of meditation. It is not a matter of getting into a spiritual absorption, a higher trance, or anything of that nature. It's a sense of being there, and then being there providing no ground. No entertainment. Blank.

Number five, the fifth category, is *prajna,* which means "knowledge." *Jna* means "intelligence" and *pra* means "premium," "higher," "greater." That's the Sanskrit word, and the Indo-European word comes from that. [*Know, gnosis, cognition,* etc., are etymologically related to *jna.*] Prajna is the premium knowledge, the highest and greatest knowledge of all. It's premium in the sense of premium gas that you can ask for at the gas station. There is a gas shortage these days, but I'm sure there is no shortage of prajna. It's ongoing stuff. Prajna, discriminating knowledge.

Prajna, to make a further entry in our Buddhist dictionary, is a process of looking. It is the highest way of looking at reality. It is like making an acquaintance (in the sense of picking a colleague, a fellow worker). You are working hard enough so you hire your own intelligence to work with you. You create a colleagueship with yourself, you make an acquaintance to work with you— knowledge.

We run into a conflict here with the Christian tradition concerning mystical wisdom. According to the Christian tradition, or any theistic tradition, wisdom comes first and knowledge comes afterward. But in Buddhism, knowledge comes first and wisdom comes later.

Once I watched a television program on Italian classical art—
Michelangelo and Leonardo da Vinci, and so on. It was beautifully
done. It was presented by some English lord or other, who spoke
very beautifully. A point he made was that in order to understand
art in the Western world, you have to look in order to see. That is
the approach of a theistic mystical experience: look in order to see.
Seeing is regarded as a discovery; looking is the primary method.
It seems obvious: if you want to see, you have to look first. Very
sensible; very scientific. Before you draw conclusions, you gather
information with the computer. When the computer says thus-
and-such and so-and-so is the case, then you begin to see. You
look in order to see. But in the nontheistic traditions, such as
Buddhism (and at this point, the only nontheistic traditional
religion we have in this universe is Buddhism), the idea is to
see in order to look. Looking is regarded as much more important, because you can't abandon the world, you can't abandon
relationships.

First you have to see. Projections are necessary in order for you
to work with yourself. Having related with your projections
properly—clearly and thoroughly—having seen things as they
are, you start to scrutinize, you start to look. When you look, you
discover all kinds of subtle qualities of things as they are, subtleties upon subtleties, fantastic details of things as they are, fantastically colorful.

Saying that you have to see in order to look is a tantric statement. It is very subtle and very precise.

What might happen to us is: we look in order to see. We look
first and have a flash of something fantastically beautiful. We look
at something and get dazzled by it. We get dazzled and begin to
see psychedelic visions of the universe. Fantastic! Wow! Then we
are supposed to see whatever it is. But seeing isn't important
anymore, because we have already looked. We lost so many subtle
little details, because we looked. The Buddhist approach toward
perceiving phenomena is to see in order to look, not look in order
to see.

This is a definition of prajna that leads toward tantra.

Understanding this is important when it comes to translating certain terms. We translate *jnana* as "wisdom" and *prajna* as "knowledge." A lot of scholars translate *prajna* as "wisdom" or *prajnaparamita* as "wisdom gone beyond." The idea of seeing in order to look is closer to Don Juan's teaching, the American Indian approach.

First you see things, perceive things. I see a lot of faces here. Heads without glasses, heads with glasses. Then I look to see who they are. They are listening to this talk.

Castaneda talks about seeing a jackal or a coyote. Don Juan placed a white cloth somewhere, then later moved it, and in doing so removed a whole landscape. It had something to do with the coyote principle. It's very interesting, very close to tantric Buddhism. The whole thing is based on seeing. For instance, in relation to the idea of choosing a spot, a place where you are going to sit and be yourself. In doing this, once you begin to look, you become very awkward. If you see a spot, you should arrange yourself suitably in it and then begin to look. That seems to be the point in discussing prajna as a preparation for discussing tantra. The pertinent experience of prajna also takes place on the mahayana level.

Looking is demanding, if you look prematurely. But seeing is undemanding if you do it properly. The sense of well-being that we talked about takes place.

Having accomplished faith, vigor, awareness, meditation, and prajna, then we begin to become somewhat proud of ourselves. We feel good. There is a sense of well-being. We do not have to reduce ourselves to the level of bullshit. We are Mount Meru.[4] We are the great mountains of the Himalayas. We are worth being proud of. We have understood faith, energy, awareness, meditation, and knowledge. We have gone through all those with the help of the six paramitas. We now begin to feel that maybe we could stick out our necks again, once more. We are noble sons and daughters of Buddha. We *are* Buddha. We have

Buddha in us. Why should we crunch ourselves down and deform our state of being? Why don't we just expand ourselves into our perfect form, our perfect being? We have perceptions and energies and inspirations. We have everything. We have a spiritual friend, we have the teaching. We have everything. What more do we want? We have everything in this whole universe. We have everything there. We have intelligence and understanding and the materials to understand. We have everything. We can afford to extend ourselves a bit more. That is why this approach is called the mahayana, the great vehicle, the bodhisattva path.[5] It is heroic.

We beat the drum of dharma, sound the trumpet of wisdom and compassion, celebrate the feast of intelligence. It is very joyous. And the reason that it is so joyous is because the whole thing is so hopeless. It doesn't provide us with any hope. Once we become hopeful, we are taking the approach of poverty. We are adopting a penniless mentality. We are locking ourselves into the ghettos of the samsaric world.

We have an enormous sense of delight. There are wonderful things taking place in us. That is the sense of the bodhisattva path. This is also connected with tantra, because in tantra, the whole thing is based on pride, vajra pride, as we call it, indestructible pride, adamantine pride. An enormous sense of delight begins to take place. There is no room, absolutely none whatsoever, for misery.

This has nothing to do with being "love-and-lighty." We don't have to furnish ourselves with goodness, whiteness, cleanness. We don't have to adopt the conviction that finally we are good and beautiful, loving and lighting. Rather we are what we are. We are sons and daughters of noble family, in the direct line of the Buddha. We have our heritage, our lineage. We can take pride in ourselves. It's fantastic.

That is the preparation for tantra. I suppose we could talk about it in terms of looking. We have seen already; then we begin to look.

STUDENT: I didn't quite get the difference between seeing and looking. It seemed that looking involved discrimination and seeing didn't. Is that the distinction?

TRUNGPA RINPOCHE: Looking is premature discrimination, and seeing is discriminating wisdom. But you can look once you have seen.

STUDENT: How do you see if you don't, at some point or other, make the effort to look?

TRUNGPA RINPOCHE: You don't deliberately try to see. That would be looking. You perceive, you just perceive. And having perceived things as they are, as we say, you begin to find yourself looking at them. It's very much like buying an antique. You don't look at the details of the piece you want to buy. If you start looking, you're going to be a loser. You're going to make wrong decisions. If you want to be a good buyer, a competent buyer, you see the antiques. You see antiqueness. You just see it, you feel it. Seeing is feeling. Then, having seen it, you begin to look. You begin to question the state of that particular antique— whether it is worth buying, whether it has been corrupted, restored, whatever. You see the piece, then you look at it, then you buy it.

If you go to an antique auction and you look at the pieces, you make the wrong choices. You bid at the wrong time. You hit yourself, hurt yourself. When you go to an antique auction, don't look, see.

STUDENT: Seeing is more panoramic, Rinpoche?

TRUNGPA RINPOCHE: Yes.

STUDENT: It's intuition as opposed to thought?

TRUNGPA RINPOCHE: Well said.

STUDENT: If you don't get sucked into looking—you know, it does occasionally happen that you don't—and you find yourself seeing instead, at that point are you still in the five *skandhas*?[6]

TRUNGPA RINPOCHE: I think you are.

S: In?

TR: Yes, both. You are in and out.

S: Could you expand on that?

TR: You are already subject to the skandhas. But there is the possibility of being free from them at the same time.

S: In other words, it's like life and death happening continuously.

TR: Continuously, yes.

S: Do you find you yourself personally in and out of the skandhas all day long?

TR: Sure. As long as you have a body. As long as you have to shit and eat and make love.

STUDENT: The hopelessness is about certain goals, isn't it? It's not a total hopelessness about yourself.

TRUNGPA RINPOCHE: Whenever there's hopefulness about yourself, there's also a problem related to a goal. Hopelessness is hopeless all over. But there are some gaps. What's the Jewish word for that? *Chutzpa*, yes. There's still chutzpa.[7]

Believe it or not, hopelessness is encouragement. It's fantastic. From our point of view, it means we are starting on a new dimension of reality. With vigor, virya, chutzpa.

STUDENT: Isn't that because you have nothing left to defend, so you have nothing left to fight against?

TRUNGPA RINPOCHE: Yes, that's right.

S: So you can do anything you want.

TR: Precisely, sure, yes. It's your universe. It's your world. Let's celebrate.

STUDENT: But still you have to keep an awareness all along of being in an ocean of gray shit? If you began to think that you weren't in it, then you would begin to fear falling back into it. You'd be back in hope and fear again. So do you have to continue to be aware that you're in the gray shit anyhow?

TRUNGPA RINPOCHE: And take pleasure in it. I'm afraid the whole thing is as gross as that. It's far from the three *H*'s: happy, healthy, and holy.

STUDENT: Is there any separation between daily life and art in terms of seeing?

TRUNGPA RINPOCHE: No. Everybody's an artist.

STUDENT: Do you learn to trust yourself from feedback you get from people and situations around you, or does it just come from yourself?

TRUNGPA RINPOCHE: Both. You relate to situations as well, obviously; otherwise you have no reference point. Your guru is your situation as well.

STUDENT: I still don't understand about seeing and looking.

TRUNGPA RINPOCHE: Do you see me?

S: I think so.

TR: You do see me. Unless you're blind, you see me. But you haven't looked yet. Until you look, you're color-blind.

4

The Basic Body

With the preparation we have made in the foregoing talks, perhaps at this point we could discuss tantra.

Fundamentally, tantra is based on a process of trust in ourself that has developed within us, which is like a physical body. Tantra involves respect for our body, respect for our environment. Body in this sense is not the physical body alone; it is also the psychological realization of the basic ground of sanity that has developed within us as a result of hinayana and mahayana practice. We have finally been able to relate with the basic form, the basic norm, basic body. And that body is what is called *tantra*, which means "continuity," "thread." That body is a sense of a working base that continues all through tantric practice. Thus tantric practice becomes a question of how to take care of our body, our basic psychological solidity, our solid basic being. In this case, the solidity is comprised of sound, sight, smell, taste, feeling, and mind. Body here is the practitioner's fundamental sanity. The practitioner has been able to relate with himself or herself to the extent that his or her basic being is no longer regarded as a nuisance. One's basic being is experienced as highly workable and full of all kinds of potentialities. On the tantric level, this sense of potential is called *vajra*, which means, "adamantine," or "diamond," or "indestructible." A sense of indestructibility and a strong continuous basic body has developed.

The notion of *mahamudra* is prominent in tantric teaching. *Maha* means "great" and *mudra* means "symbol." *Maha* here means "great" not in the sense of "bigger than a small one," but in the sense of "none better." And "better" even has no sense of comparison. It is "nonebetter," on the analogy of "nonesuch." And *mudra* is not a symbol as such. It refers to a certain existence we have in ourselves, which is in itself a mudra. Eyes are the mudra of vision and nose is the mudra of smell. So it is not a symbol in the sense of representing something or being an analogy for something. In this case, mudra is the actualization of itself. The idea is that physical activity has been seen as something workable; it is something very definite and at the same time highly charged with energy.

Particularly in Buddhist tantra, a lot of reference is made to the idea that pleasure is the way, pleasure is the path. This means indulgence in the sense perceptions by basic awakened mind. This is the mahamudra attitude. Things are seen clearly and precisely as they are. One does not have to remind oneself to be in the state of awareness. The sense objects themselves are the reminder. They come to you, they provide you with awareness. This makes awareness an ongoing process. Continuity in this sense does not need to be sought but just is.

Nobody has to take on the duty of bringing the sun up and making it set. The sun just rises and sets. There is no organization in the universe that is responsible for that, that has to make sure that the sun rises and sets on time. It just happens by itself. That is the nature of the continuity of tantra that we have been talking about. Discovering this is discovering the body.

We have a basic body, which is very intelligent, precise, sensitive to sense perceptions. Everything is seen clearly and the buddha-family principles are acknowledged. There is *vajra* intellect, *ratna* richness, *padma* magnetizing, *karma* energy of action, and the basic, solid, contemplative being of *buddha*.[1] We have acquired such a body, which is not a new acquisition. It is the rediscovery of what we are, what we were, what we might be. With the rediscovery of that, a sense of being develops, a sense of vajra pride, to use tantric language. That is, there is a sense of dignity, of joy, a sense of celebrating the sense perceptions, sense consciousnesses, and sense objects, which are part of the coloring of the mandala experience.

Now the dawn has awakened us. We see light coming from the east. We see the reflections on our window, showing that the light is coming out. It is about to be daytime, and we begin to wake up. That is the discovery of the basic body. In the tantric tradition, it is called the dawn of Vajrasattva. The basic discovery has been made that daylight is just about to come, and one is ready to work with one's sense perceptions.

We wake up and then we get out of bed. The next thing, before eating breakfast, is to take a shower. That corresponds to what is called *kriya yoga,* the first tantric yana, which is connected with cleanness, immaculateness. You have woken up and discovered that you have a body, that you're breathing and are well and alive again and excited about the day ahead of you. You might also be depressed about the day ahead of you, but still there is daylight happening, dawn is taking place. Then you take a shower. This is the kriya yoga approach to life, which has to do with beautifying your body, taking care of your body, that is, the basic body we've been talking about.

The basic idea of kriya yoga is to purify our being of anything unnecessary. Such dirt does not provide any necessary steps toward enlightenment, but is just neurosis. Here of course we do not mean physical dirt. This is a psychological, psychosomatic type of dirt. It is neither transmutable nor workable. So we jump in the shower.

You can't take a shower with fire and you can't take a shower with earth or air. You have to take a shower with water, obviously.

In this case water is the basic crystallization of one's consciousness of waterness, the water element, which is connected with basic being. The chillness of water, the coldness of water, and its sparkliness are also a process of cleaning oneself, cleaning one's body. When you take a cold shower you wake up. You're less sleepy when the water from a cold shower pours over you. So this is also a waking-up process as well as a cleansing one.

You can't take a shower with just water pouring on your body. You also have to use soap of some kind. The soap that you use in this case is mantras, which go between your mind and your body. Mantras are an expression of unifying body and mind. The Sanskrit word *mantra* is composed of *mana,* which means "mind," and *traya,* which means "protection." So the definition of *mantra* is "mind protection." Here protecting does not mean warding off evil but developing the self-existing protection of beingness. You are proclaiming your existence. You proclaim that you are going to take a shower because you have soap and water and body there already. Water as a symbol is related with consciousness in general; and body is the thingness, the continuity of thisness, solid basic sanity; and mantra is the tune, the music you play. When you dance, you listen to music. And you dance in accordance with the music.

At a certain point, mantra becomes a hang-up. It becomes another form of dirt. Like soap. If you don't rinse it off, soap becomes a hang-up, a problem, extra dirt on your body. So you apply the soap thoroughly and then you rinse it off with water.

The idea here is that mantra is the communicator. You make a relationship between the elements and basic sanity. The elements are the sense perceptions, the projections. This is the water. The projector is your state of mind. That which relates the projection and the projector is the energy that the mantra brings. When communication between those two—or rather those three, including the energy of mantra—have happened properly, then the soap—the mantra—has already fulfilled its function. Then you have a rinse. You take a further shower to clean away the soap, clean away the method. At some point the methodology itself becomes a hang-up, so you rinse it away.

Having brought mind, body, and energy together properly, one begins to develop the appreciation of one's basic being further. Your body is already clean, immaculate and beautiful.

Now we come to the next situation, which is putting on clean clothes. That corresponds to the next yana, *upa yoga*—putting clean clothes on your naked body, which has been beautifully cleaned and dried and is in absolutely good condition. Upa yoga is basically concerned with working with action. Action here is connected with fearlessness. You are no longer afraid of relating with sense perceptions, sense pleasures, at all. You are not ashamed of putting a beautiful garment on your body. You feel you deserve to put on beautiful clothes, clothes that are beautifully cleaned and pressed, straight from the dry cleaners. The action of upa yoga is further excellent treatment of one's body, one's basic sanity.

There is a need to be clothed, rather than presenting oneself naked all the time. Exposing one's body without clothes becomes purely showmanship, chauvinism. It becomes another form of ego-tripping. So the body has to be wrapped in the beautiful garment of action. This involves a sense of awareness. Every action you take is noticed; you have awareness of it. None of the actions you take is a threat to your basic sanity. Every action you take in your life situation is highly workable—there's no conflict between the mind and the body at all. In fact, your action is another way of glorifying the beauty of your body.

This kind of appreciation of action is not a matter of watching yourself act, but rather of taking pride in your basic being in action. You don't have a prefabricated attitude; your action is spontaneous action. In this case the point of action is dealing with emotions. Aggression arises, passion arises, jealousy arises—let them be as they are. Purified aggression is energy, purified passion is compassion, purified ignorance is wisdom, inspiration. Your clean body is the best of your existence. On top of that you put clean clothes, which are a further adornment of your body. This is the action aspect. There is some sense of reality at this point, and that reality is that you are no longer afraid to perform your actions. You are no longer afraid of your emotions at all. The emotions are further fuel for your inspiration.

The next tantric yana is *yoga yana.* You have bathed and put on clean clothes, and you look magnificent. You have realized your own beauty, but putting on clean clothes does not express it fully. You should take a further step, which is to put on ornaments— a beautiful necklace, beautiful rings, beautiful bracelets. Adorning your body in this way is a further way of taking care of it and appreciating its beauty, a further way of celebrating the continuity of your basic sanity. That is the yoga yana.

The sense of cleanness and the sense of being beautifully clothed produce the sense of ornament. They are a definite statement of the purity of basic sanity. In putting on these ornaments, you begin to associate yourself with the buddhas, the *tathagatas,* the bodhisattvas of the higher realms. You put on crowns and tiaras, earrings and necklaces. You behave like a king or queen on the throne. There is a complete sense of trust, a complete sense of the obviousness of your basic sanity. That is why the Buddhist tantra is pleasure-oriented.

The pleasure orientation is very important, very powerful, and very basic. If you are not pleasure-oriented, you can't understand tantra. You have to be pleasure-oriented, because otherwise you are pain- and misery-oriented. But this is not a psychological trick of convincing yourself through positive thinking. It is an obvious, reasonable, and real thing. When you treat yourself well, you feel good. When you feel good, you dress yourself in good clothes and adorn yourself with beautiful ornaments. It is a very natural and basic way of relating to oneself.

Main qualities of tantra that come out here are basic trust and basic elegance. Elegance here means appreciating things as they are. Things as you are and things as they are. There is a sense of delight and of fearlessness. You are not fearful of dark corners. If there are any dark, mysterious corners, black and confusing, you override them with your glory, your sense of beauty, your sense of cleanness, your feeling of being regal. Because you can override fearfulness in this way, tantra is known as the king of all the yanas. You take an attitude of having perfectly complete and very rich basic sanity.

Ordinarily, this is very hard to come by. When we begin to appreciate our richness and beauty, we might get trapped in ego-tripping, because we no longer have enough hinayana and mahayana discipline related to pain and hopelessness. Pain and hopelessness have to be highly emphasized, if possible to the level of 200 percent. Then we become tamed, reduced to a grain of sand. The saint knows that he is a grain of sand and therefore is no longer afraid of ornamenting himself with all kinds of beautiful things. There is a sense of dignity, of sophistication, a sense of celebration. So one of the basic points of tantra is to learn how to use pleasure fully.

Here we are not just talking about sexual pleasure. We're not just talking about the pleasure of being rich, or about pleasure in terms of getting high in a cosmic way. We are talking about pleasure in the sense that everything can be included. There is a sense of reality involved in pleasure. There is a sense of truth in it. As we said in talking about mahamudra, it is nonesuch, nothing better. It's self-existingly great, not in a comparative sense. As it is, it is great and dynamic.

STUDENT: It seems that it could be misleading to have even an intellectual understanding of this tantric material, because it would make you want to get out of your pain and suffering. So what use is it at this point?

TRUNGPA RINPOCHE: You cannot get into it unless you have a good and real understanding of pain and hopelessness.

Without that, you are nowhere near it. It would be misleading if we presented it right at the beginning and you had no idea at all of hinayana and mahayana. That would be misleading and very dangerous. You would turn into an egomaniac. But once you have an understanding of the necessity and simplicity of pain and the necessity and simplicity of compassion of the bodhisattva's path, you can begin to look into other areas. Hinayana and mahayana are necessary and very important.

STUDENT: Rinpoche, what is the relationship between negativity and the energies that are transformed into the five wisdoms?[2] I've been becoming more aware of the energy of negativity and how alive it is, but I don't see where it fits into the pattern of the five wisdoms.

TRUNGPA RINPOCHE: The whole point is that within itself, negativity is self-existing positive energy. If you have a really clear and complete understanding of negative energy, it becomes workable as a working base, because you have basic ground there already. Do you see what I mean?

S: No.

TR: Negative energy is no longer regarded as threatening. Negative energy is regarded as fuel for your fire, and it is highly workable. The problem with negative energy is that negative energy does not enjoy itself. It doesn't treat itself luxuriously—sybaritically, one might say. Once the negative energy begins to relate to itself sybaritically in its own basic being, then negative energy becomes a fantastic feast. That's where tantra begins to happen.

S: Okay. So much for negativity in itself. What then is the relationship to the five wisdoms?

TR: The five wisdoms begin to act as the clear way of seeing your negativity. In mirrorlike wisdom, vajra, aggression is seen as precise, clear-cut intellect. The wisdom of equanimity, ratna, is related with a sense of indulgence and richness; at the same time, everything is regarded as equal, so there's a sense of openness. In discriminating awareness, padma, passion is seen as wisdom in that passion cannot discriminate itself anymore, but this wisdom does perceive it discriminatingly. In the wisdom of the fulfillment of action, karma, instead of being speedy, you see things as being fulfilled by their own means, so there is no need to push, to speed along. In the wisdom of *dharmadhatu,* all-encompassing space, which is related with the buddha family, rather than just seeing stupidity, you begin to see its all-encompassingness, its comprehension of the whole thing.

The wisdoms become a glorified version of the emotions, because you are not a miser. One of the problems is that in relating with the samsaric emotions, we behave like misers; we are too frugal. We feel that we have something to lose and something to gain, so we work with the emotions just pinch by pinch. But when we work on the wisdom level, we think in terms of greater emotions, greater anger, greater passion, greater speed; therefore we begin to lose our ground and our boundaries. Then we have nothing to fight for. Everything is our world, so what is the point of fighting? What is the point of segregating things in terms of this and that? The whole thing becomes a larger-scale affair, and ego's territory seems very cheap, almost inapplicable or nonexistent. That is why tantra is called a great feast.

STUDENT: Is the thing that prevents us from relating to the world in a tantric way right now the fact that we have a sense of self? Are you saying that we have to go through the hinayana and the mahayana first in order to break down our sense of self so that we can relate to tantra?

TRUNGPA RINPOCHE: If you think on a greater scale as vajrayana, or tantra, does, you have no idea of who is who and what is what, because no little areas are kept for a sense of self. Mahayana works with more developed people, hinayana with people who are less developed but still inspired to be on the path.

Each time they relate with the path, they lose a pinch of self, selfishness. By the time people get into vajrayana, the selfishness doesn't apply anymore at all. Even the path itself becomes irrelevant. So the whole development is a gradual process. It is like seeing the dawn, then seeing the sunrise, then seeing the sun itself. Greater vision develops as we go along.

STUDENT: How can you have a sybaritic relationship with negativity?

TRUNGPA RINPOCHE: That's the greatest of all.

S: I'm sure it is, but I don't understand it.

TR: It's like putting seasoning on your food; if you don't, you have a bland meal. You add color to it, and it's fantastic. It's very real and alive. You put salt and spices on your dish, and that makes it a really good meal. It's not so much a sense of indulgence as of appreciating the meal.

STUDENT: So far in this seminar, you have skirted the use of the word *shunyata*.[3] I was wondering about the shunyata experience, which you have characterized in the past as appalling and stark. How does that relate with the sense of isness or being? I had a nihilistic feeling about shunyata. It seemed very terrifying and claustrophobic, whereas the idea of isness seems very comfortable and expansive.

TRUNGPA RINPOCHE: Isness feels good because you know who you are and what you are. Shunyata is terrifying because you have no ground at all; you are suspended in outer space without any relationship at all to a planet.

S: Shunyata is characterized in some literatures as an ultimate point, a final attainment.

TR: That's a misunderstanding, if I may say so. Shunyata is not regarded as an ultimate attainment at all. Shunyata is regarded as no attainment.

STUDENT: I'm wondering about the transition to tantra from the earlier discipline. It seems one might get hung up on the hinayana and mahayana. The hopelessness begins to have a kind of dignity, and you might get attached to it. It seems to be a very abrupt kind of transition, and it could be very hard to switch over.

TRUNGPA RINPOCHE: You are able to switch over because of your sense of sanity. You are no longer interested in whether the different yanas are going to be kind to you or unkind. You don't care anymore. You are willing to face the different phases of the various yanas. And you end up with vajrayana.

S: That takes a lot of bravery.

TR: That is the whole point. Relating with the *samaya* vow and the vajra guru takes a lot of discipline and a lot of bravery.[4] Even the high-level bodhisattvas supposedly fainted when they heard the message of vajrayana.

STUDENT: When you reach the point of transition between mahayana and vajrayana, do you have to give up your cynicism about the teachings and the teacher and about yourself that you have during hinayana and mahayana?

TRUNGPA RINPOCHE: I think so. At that point you become very clear, and cynicism becomes self-torture rather than instructive and enriching. At that point, it is safe to say, there is room for love and light. But it is sophisticated love and light rather than simple-minded lovey-lighty.

5

The Crazy-Wisdom Holder and the Student

We are going to try to go further with our understanding of vajrayana, or tantra. Something has been missing so far in our discussion of tantra. The tantric experience can only come about through a transmission from your guru, from a *vidyadhara* (which means a holder of crazy wisdom). Such a transmission can take place but involves enormous trust and enormous sacrifice. This sense of trust and sacrifice can come about at the time of receiving an abhisheka.

Abhisheka is a Sanskrit term that is usually translated "initiation." But initiation here is not just the idea of being accepted into a tribe by going through a certain ceremony. Here there is a sense of complete and total surrender. Surrendering in this way is very unreasonable from an ordinary point of view; but this sacrifice and the bond that arises from it have to be established before we can trust the universe as a potentially enlightened situation. From the tantric point of view, we have to go through this in order to be enlightened. And in order to get enlightened, one has to go through tantric training in any case. And enormous surrendering and enormous trust are involved.

Trust on this level means one cannot maintain one's ego. One cannot maintain one's basic existence as "myself." This self has become completely dedicated, it has completely opened up in surrendering to the world created by the guru. The world that the guru creates is not particularly a pleasant one. It might be very unpleasant, horrific. It might also be beautiful at the same time. The reason the world created by the guru tends to be an irritating one is that the guru goes beyond the role of spiritual friend at this point and begins to act as a dictator. He minds your business completely; he minds every inch of your life.

Your guru has the ability to do such a thing, because he knows every inch of your life, of your state of consciousness. He knows the tiniest fragments of your subconscious gossip, he knows all the little freckles in your mental functions. The guru has a complete understanding of all this. Therefore you are highly exposed, fully exposed.

For this reason, the tantric tradition is considered very dangerous. The traditional format is that you can either make love to your guru as a divine being or kill him. The analogy is that of a snake in a bamboo tube. When you put a snake in a bamboo tube, the snake has to face either up or down. Relating with the guru is very powerful, too powerful. It is too much having somebody mind your business in that fashion. From that point of view, it is extremely horrific. Nevertheless, at the same time it is an extremely delightful gift.

Tantric transmission cannot take place without a guru, without a spokesman of the mandala perspective. That is a very basic point that we should be very clear about. Entering tantra is hellish, shall we say. When the guru begins to manifest himself as somebody minding your business 200 percent, you are bound to feel extraordinarily claustrophobic. He not only minds your business, he minds the business of your business. He sees inside out, outside in. This is a very powerful and a very paranoid situation.

Without the guru's consent, without his acknowledgment of

you as a good vessel for the vajrayana, you don't get anything out of it at all. The guru acts as a channel for both creative and destructive happenings. He can destroy you instantly or instantly build you up. And this becomes very obvious, very definite.

When you approach tantra, you are approaching the magical aspect of the cosmos more and more. Magic in this sense has nothing to do with miracles as such. There is magic in the sense of certain energies, certain mysteries, that you have never tapped before. You haven't understood them, or you haven't had enough gaps in your experience to relate to them. Now you are getting into tantra, and your guru is going to initiate you into the tantric situation. You are going to begin to tap untapped areas, which we usually leave alone, which we usually daren't work with. You are getting into a very powerful situation here.

In this powerful role, the guru is referred to as he who presents the samaya vow. *Samaya* is a Sanskrit word that is translated in Tibetan as *dam tsik*. Samaya is a certain kind of bond that is like the kind of electric fence that's used to keep cows in. In this case, it is highly electrified, and if you touch it or begin to play with it, you are going to get a shock. And if you try to get out of it, you're going to get destroyed.

Destruction does not mean just death. You will end up in what's called vajra hell, which is a very powerful hell. From there, even the greatest spiritual strength cannot rescue you. That hell is neither up somewhere nor down somewhere. It is self-existing imprisonment in which your neuroses are vibrating constantly, all the time. You're trapped in that hell, and there's no remedy and no freedom at all. Pleasure and pain both become part of the imprisonment. This is why tantra is regarded as a very dangerous thing and very powerful thing to get into.

Only tantra can produce enlightenment in one lifetime. There is no other doctrine or teaching in Buddhism—including the sudden teachings of Zen, which is part of the mahayana tradition—that can deliver enlightenment in one lifetime. Tantra is the only path that enables us to attain enlightenment in one lifetime. That's true.

Getting into tantra is like taking a supersonic jet. Either it will destroy your life because it is so fast, or it will deliver you to a more advanced place. You have breakfast in Tokyo and lunch in London and dinner in New York. It's very fast and powerful. If it destroys you, you won't even have a chance to be aware of your death. You're just dead on the spot, in midair.

I am not going to explain all the aspects of how it is powerful, but you can find out.

The holder of such a doctrine is also very powerful. The holder of the doctrine is in league with death. At the same time, he is in league with Buddha. Not just an ordinary buddha, but the highest of all the buddhas, the *dharmakaya* buddha.[1] The vajra guru has enormous power over your life and complete control over the phenomenal world. He has the power to destroy you or make you an enlightened person, so it is a very powerful commitment one makes when one enters tantra.

I say this, because I want people to think thrice about getting into it, if it is even possible for them to get into it at all. It is very dangerous, and without having gone through hinayana and ma-hayana discipline, getting into it is completely out of the question. But even if you go through hinayana and mahayana, it is still dangerous to get into this vajrayana discipline, and very powerful, magnificently powerful.

Committing oneself to the vajrayana teaching is like inviting a poisonous snake into bed with you and making love to it. Once you have the possibility of making love to this poisonous snake, it is fantastically pleasurable: you are churning out antideath potion on the spot. The whole snake turns into antideath potion and eternal joy. But if you make the wrong move, that snake will destroy you on the spot.

During the early years of my teaching in America, I was very hesitant even to discuss the subject of tantra. I felt I should be conservative and keep to basic Buddhism. But the development of my students has provided me with a lot of hints [to go ahead]. They are beginning to stick their necks out and their eyes are beginning to light up. Maybe it is time to proclaim the vajrayana victory. I feel very fortunate to be able to discuss this subject. I feel we are making headway toward establishing 100 percent Buddhism in this country. Without vajrayana we don't have a head. Hinayana is the feet. Mahayana is purely heart. But Buddhism without a head is dead. Therefore I feel very happy about the possibility of sharing my understanding with you. It is like discovering a new friend. It is a very moving situation for me personally.

Nevertheless, we should be very careful of the danger we are getting into, which is enormous. I am not going to take the responsibility alone. Everyone of you is going to take the responsibility, if I may say so.

What we are discussing is one of the most secret and sacred things ever heard on this earth. It is very dangerous and powerful. People think the atomic bomb is powerful. Maybe physically it is. But we are talking about a psychological atomic bomb, which is millions of times more powerful than the physical bomb. I want you to appreciate this and become terrified of this opportunity. It's a very serious matter.

You are in a unique position having the opportunity to hear this teaching, which has never been proclaimed in this country. You should regard yourselves as very fortunate people. I am not saying this because I want to intimidate you particularly, but I want to share my responsibility with you. I feel that I can relate with every one of you, within your understanding, in terms of the complete teachings of Buddhism.

Another aspect of this is what is known as "open secret." This teaching is self-secret. You may not be able really to hear it or understand it because of your own trips, your speed, your confusion. That is a safety precaution that has already been developed. If you are not ready to hear such a thing, you don't hear it. What I have to say becomes purely gibberish.

Let us discuss the remaining three yanas of vajrayana.

The next three yanas are described as the ultimate yanas. These yanas are as far as we can go as far as Buddhism is concerned, as far as enlightenment is concerned altogether. They are called *maha-yoga* yana, *anuyoga* yana, and *atiyoga* yana. These yanas provide the most advanced teaching Buddhism can ever present to you. They are the dead-end point at which you *should* attain enlightenment. It is demanded of you: you are required to be enlightened at that point. You are guaranteed to be enlightened once you reach the highest point of atiyoga. You have no choice. And you will become enlightened in the fullest way of all.

As an analogy for the lower tantric yanas, we talked about bathing, getting dressed, and putting on ornaments. At this point, in the mahayoga yana, you no longer put on ordinary clothes: it's more like going back to ape instinct. Instead of putting on a crown of jewels and gold, now you put on a headdress of skulls. Instead of an ordinary skirt, you wear a tiger-skin skirt. Instead of an ordinary shawl, you wear a shawl of human skin. You begin to change your perspective on the world and get back to a more organic approach.

There is a hint of savagery, a hint of craziness. A hint of crazy wisdom begins to appear. Having bathed, purified, now you wear skins and bone ornaments. At this level of mahayoga yana, consciousness begins to change. Some kind of dignity begins to appear—fearlessness. Fearlessness of blood, fearlessness of earth, fearlessness of human skulls and skin. We strip away all kinds of purified levels that we have gone through before in previous yanas.

Previous yanas have taken a very genteel approach. We tried to make ourselves into an emperor or king. We bathed, we wore beautiful clothes and jewelry of all kinds. Now we develop a sense of reality of a different nature. Neurosis as such is no longer regarded as bad at all. It is regarded as an ornament, a delightful ornament, a real ornament. We can wear such ornaments, we can adorn ourselves with all sorts of neuroses that we have. This is a fantastic proclamation of sanity in fact.

This approach explains why vajrayana is very dangerous, very freaky. Nevertheless, here it is. At this point, we are willing to swim in the shit pile once again, willing to adorn ourselves with bones and skulls and skins. It is very organic. We might even say it is macrobiotic in the ultimate sense. We begin to realize, totally without fear, that we are divine beings.

The next yana is anuyoga yana. Here the sense of indulgence just described has become a trip. Abiding in the fermented manure of neurosis becomes a problem. Maybe we have indulged ourselves too much in that organic trip. Now we don't even care about that. We take off our costumes, strip. There is no need to dress up as vampires or imitate them. We begin to lose that kind of perspective. We begin to relate more with our heart and brain. *The Tibetan Book of the Dead* describes how the wrathful herukas come out of your brain and the peaceful herukas come out of your heart. This takes place now. More coordination is developed between the vajra type of heart and brain. You develop an enormous sense of being the conqueror of the whole universe. You transcend apeness altogether, or maybe you become a transcendental ape. It is very powerful. You see a panoramic openness and there is a fantastic sense of already having conquered. The conquering has already taken place and you're just revealing it.

The next and last level is atiyoga yana. At this level you don't need any kind of outfit at all. Dressing or undressing is irrelevant. Once again you expose your naked body. No clothes at all, none whatsoever. You don't even have to bathe anymore—you are what you are. The only relationship that you have at this point is to your sense perceptions of sight, sound, smell, touch, and taste. Those sense perceptions become guidelines. When you hear a sound, you relate with that very simply as part of a reminder. When you see colors, you see them that way, very simply. This is an extraordinarily high level of perception.

There we are. We have come back to where we were, back to square one. We realize that the journey never need have been made. All the journeys are a way of fooling ourselves. The journey becomes an endless journey, so there is no point in making journeys at all.

STUDENT: Rinpoche, you talked a great deal about the dangers that attend the vajrayana path. I am very puzzled by that, since the whole exercise is supposed to be about getting out of and annihilating ego, and in that case, what dangers can there be? As I see it, the only dangers there can be would relate to what's left of the ego.

TRUNGPA RINPOCHE: You said it. The only danger is getting back to ego and ego's being fortified by all kinds of techniques that you acquired.

S: I read a *chö* ritual in which you offer yourself, your flesh and your bones, to the hungry ghosts.[2] And apparently there's a possibility you might freak out, but that is a danger only to ego.

TR: The danger is that, having performed such a sacrifice, you might feel self-congratulatory about this magnificent act of yours.

STUDENT: What you said about atiyoga seems to have been that you see what you see and you hear what you hear. But it seems to me that we can do that right now.

TRUNGPA RINPOCHE: Sure, we could do it right now, but we don't want to believe in that. Therefore we need a path to lead us to that.

S: We need to develop courage, get rid of doubt?

TR: You need some kind of feeling that you have put in enough energy to arrive at that point.

STUDENT: You spoke of the vajrayana path as one that could lead to enlightenment in this lifetime. Yet in the bodhisattva vow, we vow not to enter enlightenment until all sentient beings have become enlightened. That seems to present a contradiction.

TRUNGPA RINPOCHE: I don't think so at all. That's the trick of the mahayana path; it helps you to give up. You're not going to attain enlightenment at all; you're going to work with sentient beings. And the idea in vajrayana is that you're going to attain enlightenment in one lifetime. Both work together. In mahayana, the idea that you're not going to attain enlightenment cuts your speed, your ambition. In the vajrayana, you develop pride, vajra pride, and dignity. Actually, both amount to the same thing. *You* can't become buddha in any case at all. Youless, unyou, nonyou, is going to attain enlightenment. That logic holds true all the way along. *You* can't attain enlightenment. Maybe nonyou can attain enlightenment. Good luck!

STUDENT: I think you said you can only get enlightened by going through tantric transmission. Have enlightened people from the Zen tradition gone through tantric transmission?

TRUNGPA RINPOCHE: In some cases. Sure. I think so.

S: In that case, would you say that Suzuki Roshi was a tantric master?

TR: Absolutely. Good for him.

STUDENT: You suggest thinking thrice. About what? What's the other choice besides the path?

TRUNGPA RINPOCHE: Nothing.

STUDENT: Have you experienced vajra hell?

TRUNGPA RINPOCHE: Sure. But I'm not in it. I experienced enough to tell people what it's about. Which is very hair-raising.

S: But you said that once you got in, no amount of spiritual strength could get you out again.

TR: Yes. True.

S: So you're still in it, then.

TR: You can experience a glimpse of it. But once you get into it, nobody else can rescue you. You're stuck there.

STUDENT: You said that the hinayana and mahayana were prerequisites for tantric practice. You also labeled the American Indians' spirituality tantric. But the American Indians haven't heard of hinayana and mahayana. How does that work?

TRUNGPA RINPOCHE: Very simple. The terms don't matter, really. The American Indians have an equivalent discipline of basic sanity in their domestic affairs and in their tribal life. You know: be on the earth, learn how to cook a good meal on a fire, learn how to share with your fellow tribesmen. It's very simple. They don't have to relate with the terms *hinayana* and *mahayana,* which are purely labels.

S: Okay. You say tantra is the only way to attain enlightenment in this lifetime. How can we know what we've been doing in previous lifetimes?

TR: In previous lifetimes, you may have been working toward this. Maybe that's why you're here. Maybe that's why you're one of the fortunate persons who has had the opportunity to hear the dharma properly. Maybe in a previous life you were a good cat who heard the dharma. Or maybe you were a dumb kid who heard the dharma at his parents' knee. And now you're here. It could be anything. But there is no reason why you are not here, because you are here.

STUDENT: At what level do you transcend birth and death?

TRUNGPA RINPOCHE: At the level of no speed. Speed is karmic relational action.

STUDENT: Rinpoche, why are you telling us this?

TRUNGPA RINPOCHE: This what?

S: This doctrine that we can't understand.

TR: The point is, if you can't understand it, that's the beginning of your understanding.

S: Yes, you could tell us about something that's only one or two steps ahead of where we are and we still wouldn't understand it.

TR: But it's still good. It holds true because you don't understand it. The point here is that you have to tap your own potential. If there were no possibility of that, you wouldn't be here. You might even fall asleep on the spot. I'm telling you these things for the very reason that you have not fallen asleep here.

6

Alpha Pure

As we said at the beginning, the journey through the nine yanas is a process of rediscovering oneself. As you move along the path, you have a feeling of particular locations. You are traveling through a dense forest or through heavy snow; you are climbing mountains or crossing fields; you encounter rainstorms and snowstorms. You have to stop each night to eat and sleep, and so on. All those experiences make up your journey. In a sense we could say that the rainstorms are your rainstorms, the snowstorms are your snowstorms, and the dense forests are your dense forests. It's your world. As you move through the nine yanas, it is yourself that you are rediscovering—more and more clearly.

At the beginning there is a vague idea that something is not quite right. There is something wrong with oneself. Things are questionable, and one begins to look into the question, to relate with the pain, the chaos and confusion. That is the hinayana level. Then at a certain stage some of the answers that arise out of the search begin to create further hunger, further curiosity. One's heart becomes more and more steeped in the teachings. Then the mahayana experience of intense dedication to the path begins to take place. Dedication to the path in this case also means compassion, a loving attitude toward oneself and others. One begins to find one's place in the universe, in this world. Being on the bodhi-sattva path is finding one's place and one's sense of dedication in this universe. At that point, the universe is not threatening or irritating anymore. This is true for the very simple reason that one has developed a style for working with the universe; meditation in action has begun to develop.

As you go on then, you rediscover the brand-new world of tan-tra. An enormous surprise takes place. You recognize the magical aspect of the universe, which means yourself as well as everything else. You rediscover the redness of red, the blueness of blue, the whiteness of white, and so on. You rediscover the meaning of pas-sion and the meaning of aggression, their vividness, their alive-ness, and also their transcendental quality. Rediscovering this new world is the vajrayana path.

At that point, not only do you realize the meaning of pain and confusion, and not only do you realize you have a place in the world, but you also develop a sense of dignity. In fact, you are the emperor of the universe, the king of the world. Your sense of dig-nity is related to the experience that you have an enormous place in this world. In fact, you are the maker of the world.

As the tantric experience develops through the lower tantras to the higher tantras, even the notion of being the emperor of the universe becomes unnecessary. You are the universe. You have no reference point, none at all. Everything is on the level of complete oneness. In higher tantric terms, this is known in Tibetan as *kadak*. *Ka* is the first letter of the Tibetan alphabet, *dak* means pure. So it means "pure right at the beginning," or you might say "alpha pure." Purity in this case has nothing to do with the rela-tive reference point of pure as opposed to impure. Purity here has the sense of being really without comparison to anything, without any relative reference at all. That seems to be the state of develop-ment we are working toward. That, finally, is the level of the *maha ati* teachings, in which there is no reference point, none whatso-ever. Therefore, in that state we find millions of reference points everywhere, which do not conflict with each other. Therefore we become precise and open, very general and very specific at the same time. That is the state of enlightenment, if it can be described at all in words. That's a sort of finger painting of the enlightenment idea.

The whole journey that we have discussed has its roots in overcoming spiritual materialism to begin with, then developing friendship toward oneself and others, and finally developing vajra pride, or a sense of dignity.[1] Those three steps are the general guidelines for the hinayana, mahayana, and vajrayana, or tantra. And those experiences cannot come about without a teacher or master to begin with, on the hinayana level; a spiritual friend who minds one's business intensely on the bodhisattva or mahayana level; or, on the vajrayana level, a vajra master or vajra guru, who holds one's life strings in his hand.

There is a story about the abhisheka that the great tantric master Padmasambhava received from Shri Simha, the great sage of maha ati. Shri Simha reduced Padmasambhava to the form of the letter HUM. Then he ate it, he put it in his mouth and swallowed it. And when Padmasambhava came out the other end of Shri Simha, that completed his abhisheka. This is an example of the action of the vajra master. He is more than a teacher alone, more than a spiritual friend. The vajra master eats you up and shits you out, having completely processed you in his vajra body. That is the kind of power we're talking about. Without such a relationship, without this kind of communication, vajrayana cannot be presented. Without this, one cannot even come near to understanding it. So relationships with the various levels of teacher are definitely requirements for progressing on the path.

Then, of course, there is the practice of meditation, which is another important part of the journey. One must practice meditation on the hinayana level in order to develop the basic sanity of relating to one's mind as a working basis. The *satipatthana* methods of mindfulness developed in the Theravada tradition are very

powerful and important.[2] The methods developed in the Sarvas-
tivadin hinayana tradition that exists in Tibet, Japan, and China
are identical.

When I was in India, I discussed meditation techniques for
awareness practice with a Burmese master who was the disciple of
a very great Burmese meditation teacher. When I told him about
the *vipashyana* meditation technique that we used in Tibet, he
shook his head and asked me, "When did you go to Burma?"[3] So
the methods seem to be identical.

It is necessary to begin at the beginning with the hinayana
practice. Without that, we do not develop proper sense perception, so to speak. We have to have good eyesight and good hearing to read and listen to the teachings. And we have to have a
good body in order to sit and meditate. Good sense perceptions
here mean sense perceptions that are no longer distorted. We can
have real understanding, no longer distorted by neurosis. That is
absolutely necessary; there's no other way at all, according to
Buddha anyway.

Having that solid rock bed for a foundation, that solid, sane,
open, fresh ground, you can begin to build, to put up walls. That
corresponds to the mahayana discipline of the six paramitas and
friendliness to oneself and others. This gives us a sense of direction
about how to act as good citizens, which is the bodhisattva path.
After one has become a good citizen, there is an enormous possibility of becoming a genius. Basic sanity has developed and a
proper lifestyle has been established. There are no hassles, no obstacles at all. Then you become a genius, which is the vajrayana
level.

You become a fantastic artist, musician, sculptor, or poet. You
begin to see the workings of the universe in its ultimate, last details. You are such a genius that you see everything completely.
That's the final level.

This genius is described as jnana, wisdom. There are five types
of genius, five wisdoms. There is mirrorlike wisdom, which is clar-

ity. There is the wisdom of equality, which is seeing everything at once in a panoramic vision. There is the wisdom of discriminating awareness, which is seeing details on an ultimately precise level. There is the wisdom of all-accomplishing action, in which speed does not have to be included in one's working situation, but things fall into your pattern. Then there is the fifth wisdom, the wisdom of dharmadhatu, or all-encompassing space, which develops enormous basic sanity and basic spaciousness in the sense of outer space rather than space that is related to the reference point of any planet. That is the kind of cosmic level of genius that we find in the vajrayana.

I suppose this seminar cannot be any more than a teaser for you. But at least you should know that millions of great people have been produced by this path; and not only have they been produced, but they all say the same thing. They've all gone through the same process that is being presented here. And we are not excluded from the possibility of becoming one of them. According to the Buddha, one out of every four people in the sangha becomes enlightened.

What we have done very roughly in this seminar has been to give a complete description of the path from the beginning stages to enlightenment. I hope you will have a sense of aspiration and feel joyful about what we discussed. The other possibility is that you might feel depressed, because you have heard about so many possibilities and good things, but none of them seem to apply to you. Well, okay, be that way—and use your depression as realization of the truth of suffering. Then you will have accomplished the first step already. Or if you are inspired, then buddha fever, the fever of buddha nature, has already possessed you. So let it be that way. It seems that whatever we do, we can't go wrong.

STUDENT: I have a question about inspiration or motivation. It seems that in the hinayana, the motivation is suffering. In mahayana at some point this is transformed into compassion, so that one continues because one has a sense of working, not for oneself, but for all beings. But, going beyond that, I don't understand the motivation or inspiration for vajrayana. Why would one go further?

TRUNGPA RINPOCHE: One of the interesting points about vajrayana is that it does not need to be nursed. It just happens that once you have developed the fullest level of compassion as an accomplished mahayanist, you find yourself being a vajrayanist. That's the general pattern that applies. There's no particular motivation as such. The only thing is a sense of transcendental fascination with the universe and the play of its energy, its emotions, and so on. Everything is such a magnificent display of the mandala pattern, and you can't keep yourself from looking at it.

STUDENT: If mahayana is "gone-beyond" wisdom, the wisdom of the paramitas, then would going beyond that, beyond the paramitas, be vajrayana?

TRUNGPA RINPOCHE: You could say that, yes.

S: So in some sense, it's the natural conclusion of the mahayana.

TR: You could say that too, yes.

S: Thank you.

TR: Anything you say.

STUDENT: Rinpoche, where is the spirituality in tantra? It feels like tantra could be very materialistic.

TRUNGPA RINPOCHE: How is that?

S: One thing is relating to one's sense perceptions as real. Couldn't that just be spiritual materialism, perhaps? It just seems to me that after mahayana, the spirituality becomes vague.

TR: If we just started with tantra, we might end up cultivating Rudra, which is very dangerous. Tantra can only develop by going through the other yanas first, destroying all kinds of spiritual materialism.

It's very interesting: you can't say tantra is a spiritual thing exactly, nor is it a worldly thing. That's why tantra is said to transcend both samsara and nirvana. There is a term in Tibetan that Herbert Guenther translates "coemergent wisdom." The idea of coemergence here is that you are on neither side; you are not on the side of ignorance nor on the side of wisdom. Because of that, a lot of hinayanists and mahayanists panicked about tantra— because it's completely unspiritual. On the other hand, they can't say tantra is worldly, because there is nothing worldly about tantra either—because of the craziness.

STUDENT: What advice would you give for dealing with somebody who is in vajra hell?

TRUNGPA RINPOCHE: Let me go over the idea of vajra hell once again, if I may. Having heard the vajrayana teachings, instead of becoming awakened, you become deaf and dumb to the teachings. The medicine turns into poison. And there's nothing one can do for such a person. The only thing is to imprison them in a vajra den, which is vajra hell. It's like you have a prison cell made out of books about the vajrayana all around you. They imprison you. But you might be interested some time or other just in pulling one out, and maybe you might read it. Sheer claustrophobia brings some kind of hope. It is a rather horrific place to be.

S: Would an ordinary prison be any kind of comparison to vajra hell?

TR: I don't think so. It's much more than that. It's a total experience, like having cancer throughout your whole body. But you can't even die out of it. You're fed by the disease.

STUDENT: Does it have an eternal quality? You said there's no escape from it.

TRUNGPA RINPOCHE: Claustrophobia is eternity in this case. There're no windows and no doors. You can't even exist, but this threat of nonexistence becomes the food that keeps you alive.

S: There's no possibility of a future way out in terms of a bardo?

TR: *The Tibetan Book of the Dead* describes two types of advanced rebirth that can take place. Either you go up to the level of dharmakaya without a bardo experience or else you go down to vajra hell, also without a bardo experience. Because a bardo is some kind of chance or opportunity you have.

STUDENT: Would it be beneficial to try to help somebody in vajra hell?

TRUNGPA RINPOCHE: Helping doesn't particularly change the karma of that person.

S: So it's best to avoid such people?

TR: Best to leave them as they are.

S: But how does that relate to the bodhisattva vow?

TR: In taking the bodhisattva vow to save all sentient beings, you could add "except those who are in vajra hell." Even bodhisattvas can't reach the helpless.

STUDENT: Can a person in vajra hell ever get out by becoming aware of himself, say, by reading those books that make up his prison?

TRUNGPA RINPOCHE: Yes, that's the only possibility. Through sheer claustrophobia, you might be able to squeeze something out of yourself.

STUDENT: You said that at the end of this journey, there is the realization that there was never a need to make this journey at all. But at the same time, isn't the journey absolutely necessary?

TRUNGPA RINPOCHE: It is necessary in order to realize that your journey was futile. It is called a path, but it is not really a path, because you are really neither coming nor going. But still there is an illusion of a journey. That's why the various levels are called yanas, which means "vehicles." You think you are moving. But maybe it is the landscape that is moving.

STUDENT: Doesn't the analogy of vehicles also contain the idea that you are being carried by the energy of the path rather than you yourself making any progress?

TRUNGPA RINPOCHE: That is also possible. That depends on how much you are identified with the teachings personally. Once you are identified with the teachings personally, then development is sort of like wine fermenting. It ferments by itself.

STUDENT: You used the analogy of an electric fence around a cow pasture. If the cow tries to go beyond the fence, it gets a shock. There's some kind of painful situation. I take that to mean that once a person is on the path, there is some kind of safeguard that the guru, through his insight, provides. Then, in order to flip out and go to vajra hell, it is necessary to make some sort of egoistic assertion to the effect that the guru is no longer able to discriminate properly what is right and what is wrong for us. Is that what this vajra hell thing is about? And then you are left to go off on your own?

TRUNGPA RINPOCHE: Are you asking if that kind of a development is the cause of vajra hell?

S: Yes.

TR: I think so. Some sort of alienation takes place between the teacher and the student. There is the story of Rudra, one of the first persons to go to vajra hell. He and a fellow student, a dharma brother, were studying with the same master. They had a disagreement about how to interpret the master's instructions. They were taking opposite extremes in carrying out their practice, and each of them was sure that he was right. They decided to go to the teacher and ask for his comment. When the teacher told Rudra that he was wrong, Rudra became so angry that he drew his sword and killed his teacher on the spot. Then he ended up in vajra hell. It is that kind of alienation.

STUDENT: Is going to vajra hell the equivalent of attaining egohood, or are they two different things?

TRUNGPA RINPOCHE: Vajra hell is not quite complete egohood. It's still part of the journey. But when you come out of vajra hell without any realization, then you attain the real egohood, which is the state of Rudra. You turn yourself into a demon.

S: So you're not in vajra hell when you attain egohood.

TR: No, egohood seems to be quite difficult to attain. As difficult as enlightenment. Doing a really good job on it is very difficult.

STUDENT: It seems to me that some act of surrendering is definitely necessary. But is that something you can try to do, or do you just have to wait and let it happen? Is it something you have to stop trying to do?

TRUNGPA RINPOCHE: The general policy seems to be that you have to surrender artificially to begin with. You have high ideals, some inspiration about what the possibilities might be, but you can't quite click into those possibilities spontaneously at the beginning. So you have to start by creating artificial openness, by surrendering artificially. This is precisely what taking the refuge vow or the bodhisattva vow is. It is artificial actually—you are not up to it. But the commitment involved begins to have an effect on your state of being, for the very reason that you cannot wipe out your past. That artificial gesture becomes part of the landscape of your life; then something there begins to ferment, begins to work.

T W O

Nine Yanas Seminar

SAN FRANCISCO • MAY 1973

I

Suffering, Impermanence, Egolessness

The nine yanas of the Buddha's way were developed to enable people—psychologically, personally, physically—to surrender themselves to the Buddha's teaching. The nine yanas seem to be an absolute necessity. If we did not have the first yana, nothing could be achieved at all. We have to start with the first step, which is the *shravaka* yana, in which everything is looked at in terms of a human situation, a physical situation. Here the Buddha is regarded as a son of man who still had a physical obligation to this earth. He was also wise. He saw everything in our life situation as consisting of pain. But at the same time the nature of pain is characterized by impermanence, and the experiencer of the pain is regarded as nonexistent. So there are these three points: the nature of life is pain; the nature of pain is impermanent; and the experiencer of pain is nonexistent.[1]

You might ask, if the experiencer of pain is nonexistent, how come there are situations in which we feel that we do experience pain and pleasure, very solid situations? How do we know that this nonexistence is the case? If the Buddha said that being is nonexistent, how do we experience pain and how do we experience impermanence?

We simply say, "I don't know about everything else, but I still feel pain. I do feel pain. I do feel frustrated. I do feel unhappy, I really do. I don't know about the impermanence or nonexistence of my being, but I simply do experience pain, I sure do." Well, in some sense, that's great. At least you have found some relationship with the teaching. If you really do experience pain and suffering in its own way, that's wonderful, fantastic.

Are you sure, though, that you are really experiencing pain, experiencing it in the fullest way? "Well, I'm not even certain of that, but I do feel some kind of discomfort. I do experience pain when I'm pushed into a corner, but during the rest of my life, I'm not so certain whether I actually experience pain or not. I do experience pain when somebody hits me, cheats me, or insults me. Then I do feel extreme pain, discomfort, anger, and so forth. But the rest of the time I'm not so sure whether I feel pain as a continual thing happening to me. All the same, I feel that there's something hanging out that's bugging me; and I don't feel absolutely free either. Particularly when I check up on what's happening with me, I feel funny. I feel some sense of being trapped, but I don't know what it's all about. Maybe this is happening, but maybe also I'm just imagining it. I can't say. Something is happening. Sometimes I feel haunted, and sometimes I feel I'm just being silly—I should forget the whole thing. I should just go out and enjoy myself and do my own thing, whatever I want. But even if I try to do that, I can't really do it, because I still stop and look back at myself and what I'm doing. And once I begin to check what I'm doing, I feel uncomfortable. Something is bugging me somewhere. Something is happening behind my back, as if I had a huge burden that I'm carrying all the time. But I'm not sure if this is the thing that's happening to me or I'm just imagining it. Maybe I should stop thinking altogether. But I already thought of that and tried it. The more I try to shake off the watcher, the more I feel I have to make sure that I have shaken him off. I couldn't shake him off because I was being watched all the time by my shaking-off project that was happening to me."

Maybe Buddha had similar experiences, even identical ones. There was a sense of ambition to become a spiritual or religious person. Buddha went so far as to leave home. He left his parents and his wife and infant child. He fled from his palace and plunged into the world of yogic teachers, Hindu masters. But still something didn't work, because in some sense he was trying too hard, trying to become great, the greatest spiritual warrior of the century. He was trying to achieve something; he was concerned with achieving and with saving himself.

That seems to be the problem that we encounter all the time. We feel uncertain because, though we feel we know what direction we should go in, when we try to follow that direction, that itself seems to become a source of ignorance. The direction we were following seems to turn into clouds and clouds of darkness. Finally we begin to lose our sense of direction. But that seems to be the basic point: in relation to that, we discover pain, duhkha. That pain is a self-existing thing that we cannot escape. Beyond the pain, we try to find the source of the pain, the origin of the pain, but we don't find it. We find bewilderment and fogginess, uncertainty of all kinds. But that *is* the discovery of the origin of pain, which is a very important discovery indeed.

Discovering the origin of pain does not necessarily mean that we should give up hope, or that we should give up fear, for that matter. Giving up means disregarding the whole thing rather than working with it.

Pain is constantly existing. Even if we find the origin of pain, it is a constant discovery, a very powerful one. Pain exists all the time whether we feel happy or sad. The happiness is superficial; pain is behind the happiness all the time. The pain goes on constantly: the self-existing pain, the pain of self-consciousness, the pain of ambition, and so on. All of those go on all the time regardless of the superficialities of what we feel. The facade is different, but behind it is the fundamental pain that is happening constantly.

The experience of pain thrives on its own fickleness. It is like a lamp burning or a candle flame. The flame has to breathe very fast to remain solid and still. It has to get fuel from the candle as it burns. It is continuously breathing, so the stillness of the flame is based on the continuity of discontinuity. Constant death and constant birth are taking place simultaneously. We cannot hang on to life as though it were something solidly continuous like a pipe. If life wasn't changing, if life was a solid thing happening solidly, then we couldn't have pleasure and we couldn't have pain. We would be frozen into jellyfish or robots, reduced into rocks. Because we are able to experience our pain and pleasure, our highs and our lows, depressions and excitements, all kinds of things can develop in our life situations. That means that there is automatically some sense of change or shifting happening all the time.

A bridge wouldn't be built if a river was still. Because a river is dangerous and turbulent and passing all the time, because the current is happening constantly, therefore we build a bridge. Otherwise we could just put a huge boat there and walk across that. The sense of discontinuity is important. Impermanence is important.

But before getting into impermanence further, we should mention that there are different types of pain. There are three types of pain. The first is pain as a natural condition. This is the pain that is always there. Even when we are indulging in pleasure, extraordinary sybaritic pleasure—delightful, beautiful, fantastic, deep, profound pleasure, pleasure that is physical, psychological, reassuring, solid, textural—even that contains a tone of suspicion constantly. Even if we have millions of guards to protect our pleasure domain, still there is a tone of pain happening. However extraordinarily happy we may be, there is still a tone that suggests that the whole pleasurable situation might possibly be extraordinarily painful. There is a sense that we are dwelling on, digging, the pleasure for the sake of the pain or digging the pain purely for the sake of the pleasure. It feels questionable—our mind is completely intoxicated, so we are uncertain whether we are digging the pleasure to defend against the pain or digging the pain to defend against the pleasure. That is the quality of self-existing pain. Pain is definitely not fun, not particularly pleasurable.

The second kind of pain is the pain of change. You think you have pleasure happening in your existence. You feel you are involved in a real, good, solid, organic situation of pleasure. The pleasure feels extremely definite, even to the point where you no longer feel you have to defend your pleasure or compare it with pain at all. You are out on a sailboat, enjoying yourself, sunning yourself on the deck. The weather is beautiful. The sea is smooth. The wind direction is good. You had some nice food before you went out, and you have a nice companion who sparks your wit and takes care of you. It is an absolutely ideal situation. Suddenly a storm comes, a hailstorm. You don't have a chance to get yourself together, to protect yourself. Your boat is tipped over. Your wittiness is unable to continue. Instead of wit, aggression now becomes a problem. You blame your companion. You feel it is his fault, because he didn't take precautions against such a thing. You regret that you didn't have a life jacket on board. You are just about to die. You've sailed too far out into the ocean, because you wanted to be alone and enjoy your friend's companionship. You have sailed out too far for anyone to rescue you. You regret that. You have killed yourself.

That is pleasure changing to pain. By the way, the traditional analogy for that is being at your wedding party and suddenly having the house collapse due to earthquake, or whatever. That is the second type of pain. The first type was self-existing pain, within pleasure.

The third one is the pain of pain. In this case, you are already caught up in pain, extreme pain. Real, juicy, good pain. For example, you are experiencing the acute pain of just having been in an automobile accident. Your ribs have been fractured, and you can hardly breathe, let alone talk. Even if somebody makes a joke, it is painful to laugh. You are in extreme pain. Then you catch pleurisy or pneumonia. You can't talk because of your rib fracture, and now you catch pleurisy or pneumonia, and you can't even breathe without extreme pain. Or it is like having leprosy, being ridden with leprosy, and then having a car accident on top of that. Or you are already bankrupt, and then on top of that you are kidnapped, and the kidnappers demand more money.

Those three types of suffering are part of the display of impermanence. Suffering happens because impermanent situations exist. Suffering cannot exist on solid ground. Suffering has to dwell or develop in a situation, and situations can develop because situations are constantly changing. We die so that we can be reborn. We are born so that we can die. Blossoms bloom in the spring so that there will be seeds in the autumn. Then the winter gives the seeds time to adapt to the soil. Then spring comes again. The seeds are awakened after their hibernation. Having settled down to the ground, the seeds are reawakened. Then the plants grow, and there are more seeds. Then another spring comes, another summer comes, another autumn comes, and so forth. Things change constantly, always.

We think we can keep a record of things if we write them down in our notebooks. "On this particular day, such-and-such a thing happened. I heard a word of wisdom on this particular day. I'll write that down." You write that down today for the sake of what you experience now. But then you walk out of this situation and you relate with yourself tonight, tomorrow, the next day, the next week. When you read your note again after that, it is not going to speak to you as you thought it would when you wrote it down tonight, right now. The inspiration and the impact are going to change, change constantly. Let's see what happens if you write something down: that the pain of pain is acute and powerful. Then you'll walk out of this hall and spend your time: tonight, tomorrow, the next day, the next day, the next day, and so on. You will begin to develop self-consciousness concerning the fact that you wrote this thing down rather than relating to the idea or the philosophical implications that inspired you.

Things are like that constantly. Statements that we hear and things that we experience are not as solid as we would like. For that matter, even the experience of enlightened mind flashing is not all that permanent. It is a temporary situation. Fundamentally, we are distrustful people, all of us. We can't trust ourselves at all. We get one impression one moment and another impression the next, and so forth. We cannot repeat what we experienced the previous hour, thirty minutes ago—at all. We are untrustworthy persons because we are subject to impermanence.

Moreover, if we keep changing to the next subject, it's because we have no substance to hang on to. This is what we call egolessness, if I may introduce that subject as well. The notion of egolessness refers to the fact that we don't have any central headquarters. We do not have a definite thing, definite ground, to maintain—me, mine, my existence as such. We have been fooled by the play back and forth [into thinking that there is such a thing]. It's purely that we have been fooled by the back-and-forth, by impermanence, thrown back and forth between this and that, that and this, past and future, future and past. People are thrown back and forth constantly like a Ping-Pong ball. So in conclusion I would like to point out that we do not have a heavy basic solid soul or ego as we would like to have. We do not have that at all. Because of that, we are so frivolous that we are unable to grasp any teachings, any solid situation of basic sanity at all.

If we had some basic ego, a solid thing with aggression and passion happening to it, then we might be able to grasp onto that as a monumental expression of some kind. We could say: "Once I killed myself. I would like to make that into a monument, a reference point for praise. I would like to show that to other people: 'This is my monument—my having killed myself.'" But that won't work. You are not around anymore if you have killed yourself. Yet it seems that that is what we are asking for: "I have become an extraordinary person because I have given up what I was and have become what I would be, and this is my image for the future, which is independent of the present." That [making a monument out of hanging on to your projection of yourself] seems to be one of the biggest problems that has happened. So egolessness at this point means that you cannot hang on to anything; you cannot hang on to any experience.

STUDENT: Is the trouble and pain of samsara potentially the same for everybody?

TRUNGPA RINPOCHE: I think it's the same for everybody, yes. If somebody values pleasure, then pain automatically comes along with it as its shadow. If somebody asks for light, a shadow will be there along with that.

STUDENT: I thought you said that pain was there regardless of the pleasure, that it was not just a complement to the pleasure but was continuous in the background in any case.

TRUNGPA RINPOCHE: Yes, the background is also pain, painful. It is not a matter of choice; it is a constantly painful situation. But the background is also asking for an ideally pleasurable background, asking for the whole thing to be smooth. This asking for smoothness is trying to defend against roughness, which automatically invites pain.

STUDENT: We seem to be using pain for a lot of different things. I understood that the background pain is not the same as the other pain that we invite when we try to insist on pleasure.

TRUNGPA RINPOCHE: Yes, you are right. There are several types of pain. The background pain is very low key, background-ish. It has a basically paranoid quality, a quality of being haunted. Then there's the actual pain that challenges your pleasure. Then there's more actual pain [the third type], which invites chaos. It is a suicidal thing. You have one pain and you invite another pain on top of that.

STUDENT: Is understanding the pain that you call the background pain the Buddha's teaching?

TRUNGPA RINPOCHE: All the pains are teachings. That alone is nothing particularly extraordinary. But you should also realize that you were born out of pain and dwell in pain as far as the way of samsara is concerned. So any element that is related with the pain is the truth of duhkha, suffering, the first noble truth. Just experiencing the pain is not quite the point; the point is acknowledging that such pain does exist in your being. Acknowledging the pain is the teaching.

STUDENT: It's easy to acknowledge the pain. I just say, "Well, the root of everything is suffering." But it's another thing for me to be aware of the experience.

TRUNGPA RINPOCHE: You don't particularly have to stop in order to experience it. You have the experience first. That seems to be why you are here attending this seminar, which is in itself a very positive action. You have decided to come here and discuss the whole thing, which is a very inviting situation, a hopeful situation, a pleasurable one, we might even say. Your being here means that you have decided to work on your pain. That's great, wonderful. But that doesn't mean that we here are going to undermine your pain. We are going to accentuate the meaning of your pain. The teaching does not provide a possible hope, the possibility of a pleasurable situation. The teaching provides intelligence to relate with the pain.

STUDENT: Does the background pain lack coherence in the way you were talking about with the candle flame? Does the background pain exist as a kind of moment-to-moment thing, rather than—?

TRUNGPA RINPOCHE: It's always there, always there. The front part of the pain is depression, excitement, and so forth [it is more fickle]. But the background pain goes on all the time, simply because you have experience of some kind. Experience is pain. Your human functioning—any kind of intelligence that goes on in your mind—*is* pain, because you feel uncomfortable about the whole thing. Even if you have a tremendous insight to the effect that you are going to conquer the world, make yourself a million dollars, still there is something not quite fitting. There is some kind of hole somewhere that is not quite comfortable. That is the original pain. There is a very mystical experience of pain, something not quite comfortable.

STUDENT: Why do we decide to continue to exist? Some people say that the ego is body consciousness, so it seems that the body could decide to keep on living even when the ego has decided not to live anymore. But if you really decided you didn't want to be on this planet, couldn't you just leave it when your body was sleeping?

TRUNGPA RINPOCHE: You can't.

S: Why not?

TR: You can't, because you begin to notice yourself. No other logic is necessary. Because you notice yourself, you let the rest of it come along as well. Anyhow, committing suicide does not solve the whole problem. You killed yourself. There is someone watching you being killed.

S: The ego isn't body-consciousness, then?

TR: The ego is self-consciousness. And self-consciousness is automatically the relative reference point for other at the same time. In that sense, you cannot destroy the law of relativity. So you have to live.

That is precisely the idea of enlightenment: transcending the barrier between this and that [self and other]. But enlightenment does not mean suicide, killing this or that. That doesn't work. Purely removing the barrier between this and that is the only solution.

STUDENT: Is pain a kind of energy?

TRUNGPA RINPOCHE: Yes, pain is energy.

S: Then pain brings energy.

TR: If it weren't for that, I wouldn't be here. Buddhism wouldn't be here on this continent if there wasn't enough pain. Your pain has brought fantastic energy. That's why I'm here. That's why Buddhism, buddhadharma, is here. That's why tantra is here. Without pain there is no energy. That pain is an indication that you are serious, that you want to relate with your situation in the space of truth, if I may say so.

STUDENT: Rinpoche, it seems that pain brings on a certain inspiration. For example, when things get very painful, there's a shift from the background to the foreground. This means that you can be aware of the pain, and somehow that begins to change the energy. But then inspiration goes. It leaves once the pain goes back to the background. It goes back and forth again. How do you sustain the inspiration?

TRUNGPA RINPOCHE: Inspiration shouldn't be regarded as a cure or as medicine. Inspiration shouldn't be regarded as an enlightened state. The inspiration is to bring out more shit and piss and being willing to face that. If you are into that, then no doubt you will get more pain, more frustration, more inspiration, more wisdom, more insight, and more enlightenment in your life. That's up to you.

Competing with Our Projections

The first yana, shravaka yana, which we discussed yesterday, is the starting point. It is the starting point in the sense that in it we begin to realize the meaning of life; or, we might say, we discover the stuff that life consists of. Life consists of pain, transitoriness, and nonsubstantiality. Discovering that could be said to be discovering the first truth about life. You might find that rather depressing, but nevertheless, that's the way things are.

The first step, which happens in the shravaka yana, is realizing the form of manifestations, realizing the nature of manifestations; realizing the nature of sound, objects, colors, movements, and space; realizing the nature of shapes and their characteristics.

The next yana is called the pratyekabuddha yana. This means the yana or path of self-enlightenment or self-contained enlightenment. This involves starting on oneself before getting involved with anything else. As they say, "Charity begins at home." One has to start with oneself. It is because of this that the approach of hinayana as a whole has been referred to as a self-centered approach. Christianity has often looked down on Buddhism as being too self-centered. Christians have said that there isn't enough charity in Buddhism, or there aren't enough charitable organizations in Buddhism. In some sense that is the shortcoming of the hinayana.

There's too much emphasis on oneself. But on the other hand, that is the virtue of the hinayana. There's no fooling around with anything else. One does not need encouragement or reinforcement from elsewhere, from any foreign element. We don't have to introduce foreign elements in order to prove our existence. We just simply work with the stuff we have. We start right on the point where we are.

The pratyekabuddha yana could also be described as a yana of the psychological understanding of the meaning of life. In the shravaka yana, we related to the physical structure of the meaning of life. We related to impermanence and the dissatisfaction produced by impermanence; and the fact that basically things have no substance, they are empty; there is no watcher, no observer, therefore there is egolessness.

In the pratyekabuddha yana, the approach to psychological development is that of the five skandhas. [1] The first is the skandha of form. Form in this case is basic being, which is ignorance from the samsaric point of view. It is that which causes duality, the split between subject and object, between projector and projection. But at the same time that kind of ignorance is very intelligent and very definite and full of all kinds of tactics and schemes. It has already developed the scheme, the policy, of ignoring any possible threats. The meaning of ignorance here seems to be ignoring the threats of any possibilities of realizing egolessness. In other words, it means ignoring that its own game is a foolish one. In that sense, ignorance is effortless. It is a kind of natural ape instinct in which, wanting to hang on to something, we don't even have to think about hanging on to it. Ignorance holds it automatically. It senses that there are possibilities of letting go, but it doesn't want to face them. If you let go, then you no longer have pain or pleasure to occupy yourself with, so you stay on the edge of the straight path. Straightforwardness is seen, but instead of going ahead right onto the path of straightforwardness, you stay on the edge. That is basic ignorance.

It seems that we all have that tendency. We know that there are possibilities of loosening up, of freeing ourselves, but we don't really want to give in to them, because it would be too humiliating in the sense that we would no longer have any weapons to wave. We would no longer have any stuff to entertain ourselves with.

There is a sort of hunger for pain. Usually when we think of pain, we don't regard it as something we want. The conventional idea of pain is something that any sensible person would regard as undesirable. But actually and fundamentally, that's not true. There is a very profound unreasonableness that ignorance has created, which makes it so that we want to hang on to pain. At least having the experience of pain reassures us of our existence. We have a chance to play with it as though we didn't want it, which is a game. We are playing a game with ourselves.

All those schemes and projects involved in maintaining ego and pain are unconscious or subconscious ones. There is an inbuilt reaction that happens that even the watcher doesn't see. It happens on an instinctive level; therefore it is ignorance. It is a self-contained administration.

And then we have another skandha beginning to develop, which is the skandha of feeling. Feeling also is on a somewhat semiconscious level. We are beginning to be aware of ourselves, of our existence, and because of that we start to survey our territory and check our security to see whether the environment around us is threatening or welcoming or indifferent. The area around us in this sense is comprised of our basic fear or paranoia of ego's possibly losing its grip. This sends out a kind of magnetic field, and feeling is the messenger that tests out that magnetic field of ego. It tests whether the mechanism of ego will work or not, whether we will be able to survive or not.

Beyond that, a cruder level than that of the subconscious mind develops. This is the actual manifestation onto the solid level, which is perception [the third skandha]. Perception is another form of feeling but on the more active level of perceiving, of sharpening sense-consciousness. Having developed a way of detecting whether the area around us is desirable or undesirable, now we have to survey the projections more. We look to see if there is a way of seemingly changing the projections to make them constitute a more favorable situation, to make them into more favorable perceptions. This is a kind of intuition, the highest form of intuition, in which we try to see whether we can maintain ourselves or not in terms of relationships.

The next skandha is intellect, intellect in the sense of that which labels things, gives them a name and puts them into certain categories.[2] It does this in such a way that these categories fit with what we checked out by means of feeling and studied through perceptions. Now finally we make an official statement that things fit into this category or that category in relation to oneself and one's productions. This is a work of art, an intellectual one. So the intuition of perception is general sensing, and intellect is finalizing.

Then the fifth skandha is consciousness, which contains emotions, thought patterns of all kinds. Emotions come from frustration. The meaning of emotion is frustration in the sense that we are or might be unable to fulfill what we want. We discover our possible failure as something pathetic, and so we develop our tentacles or sharpen our claws to the extreme. The emotion is a way of competing with the projection. That is the mechanism of emotion.

The whole point is that the projections have been our own manifestations all along. Naturally, we have put out our own projections. We put them out as our allies, our subjects, our guards who could bring back messages and let us know what's happening. But at the same time, the ruler [the projector] is very suspicious of anything other than himself. There is the possibility that your ally might turn into your enemy; your closest friend might become your enemy; your bodyguards might assassinate you. That kind of suspicion is always happening, and because of this uncertain relationship with the projections, emotions begin to arise as another way of undermining the projections. In other words, the ruler himself has to have a weapon in case he's attacked. That is emotion.

Emotion is uncertainty regarding the projections, and the projections have also been put out by us. What we label things makes the projections. The buildings or the houses or the trees or the people as such are not the projections. What we make out of them is the projections—our version of the buildings, our version of the landscape, the people, the trees. It is the new coat of paint that we put on them, the reproductions we make of them. And there is the possibility of not being able to relate with those, since we are uncertain of ourselves [and thus uncertain of our own projections].

Basically, we are uncertain of who we are, so there is a huge, gigantic fear in the back of our minds, which is hidden very neatly behind the veil of ignorance, of ignoring. But even though it is hidden, we are still uncertain—as though there were a huge, cosmic conspiracy happening. Whether the bomb is going to explode from the inside or the outside is uncertain. But we don't talk about the inside bombs. On that side, we pretend that nothing has gone wrong at all. At least we have to have some place to sit, to live, dwell. So we decide to blame everything on the outside situation.

So that is the psychological state of the pratyekabuddha; that is his worldview on the psychological level. There seem to be two aspects to the meaning of life. There is the meaning of life from the point of view of the outside, which is characterized by the three marks of existence: pain, impermanence, and egolessness; and there is the internal way of seeing the meaning of life, which is in terms of the five skandhas.

It seems to me that we can't be charitable to anyone, even ourselves, if we do not know who we are and what we are, or who we are not and what we are not—whether we exist or not. This is a very important point to understand before we begin to practice.

We have to find out who is actually practicing and what we are practicing for.

Those two yanas, the shravaka yana and the pratyekabuddha yana, are purely hinayana. They constitute the hinayana level of philosophy and practice. The role of the hinayana in the dharma is to define life, to lay the ground, establish a foundation. That foundation is a real understanding of the practitioner and a real understanding of the basic meaning of practice.

The meditation practice in the hinayana goes right along with what we have been describing philosophically. Meditation practice at this level is establishing a relationship with yourself. That is the aim of meditation. There are various techniques for doing that. It is not a question of achieving a state of trance or mental peace or of manufacturing a higher goal and a higher state of consciousness at all. It is simply that we have not acknowledged ourselves before. We have been too busy. So finally we stop our physical activities and spend time—at least twenty minutes or forty-five minutes or an hour—with ourselves.

The technique uses something that happens in our basic being. We just choose something very simple. Traditionally, this is either the physical movement of walking or sitting or breathing. Breathing seems to have the closest link with our body and also with the flux of emotions and mental activities. Breathing is used as the basic crutch. This is the hinayana way of relating with oneself to begin with.

When we talk about making a relationship with ourselves, that sounds quite simple. But in fact it is very difficult. The reason we are unable to relate with ourselves is that that there is fundamental neurosis that prevents us from acknowledging our existence—or our nonexistence, rather. We are afraid of ourselves. However confident or clever or self-contained we may be, still there is some kind of fear, paranoia, behind the whole thing.

Neurosis in this case is inability to face the simple truth. Rather than do that, we introduce all kinds of highfalutin ideas—

cunning, clever, depressing. We just purely bring in as much stuff as we like. And that stuff that we bring in has neurotic qualities. What "neurotic" finally comes down to here is taking the false as true. The illogical approach is regarded as the logical one. So just relating with ourselves in meditation practice exposes all this hidden neurosis.

That may sound fantastic. We might think there has to be some secret teaching, some semimagical method—that we can't expose ourselves just by doing something simple like breathing or just sitting and doing nothing. But strangely enough, the simpler the techniques, the greater the effects that are produced.

The sitting practice in hinayana is called *shamatha*. This literally means "dwelling on peace" or "development of peace," but let us not misunderstand *peace* in this case. It does not refer to tranquillity in the sense of a peaceful state. *Peace* here refers to the simplicity or uncomplicatedness of the practice. The meditator just relates with walking or breathing. You just simply be with it, very simply just be with it.

This technique is especially designed to produce exquisite boredom. It is not particularly designed to solve problems as such. It is very boring just to watch one's breathing and sit and do nothing; or walk, not even run, but just walk slowly. We may think we have done that many times already. But usually we don't just breathe and sit and walk. We have so many other things happening at the same time, millions of projects on top of those things. But in this case we relate to the boredom, which is the first message of the nonexistence of ego.

You feel as if you are in exile. You are a great revolutionary leader. You had a lot of power and schemes and so on, but now you are in exile in a foreign country and you're bored. Ego's machinations and administration have no place in boredom, so boredom is the starting point of realization of the egoless state. This is very important.

Then at some point, within the state of boredom, one begins to entertain oneself with all kinds of hidden neuroses. That's okay, let them come through, let them come through. Let's not push neurosis away or sit on it. At some point, even those entertainments become absurd—and you are bored again. Then you not only draw out the discursive, conceptual side of hidden neurosis, but you begin to become emotional about the whole thing. You're angry at yourself or at the situation you managed to get yourself into. "What the hell am I doing here? What's the point of sitting here and doing nothing? It feels foolish, embarrassing!" The image of yourself sitting on the floor and just listening to your breathing—that you let yourself be humiliated in this way—is terrible! You are angry at the teacher and the circumstances, and you question the method and the teaching altogether.

Then you try more questions, seeking out another kind of entertainment. This involves believing in mystery. "Maybe there is some kind of mystery behind the whole thing. If I live through this simple task, maybe it will enable me to see a great display of higher spiritual consciousness." Now you are like a frustrated donkey trying to visualize a carrot. But at some point that becomes boring as well. How many times can you seduce yourself with that? Ten times, twenty times? By the time you have repeated the same thing seventy-five times, the whole thing becomes meaningless, just mental chatter.

All those things that happen in sitting meditation are relating with ourselves, working with ourselves, exposing neuroses of all kinds. After you have been through a certain amount of that, you master the experience of breathing in spite of those interruptions. You begin to feel that you actually have a real life that you can relate to instead of trying to escape or speed [along without having to connect with it]. You don't have to do all those things. You can be sure of yourself, you can really settle down. You can afford to slow down. At this point you begin to realize the meaning of pain and the meaning of egolessness and to understand the tricks of ignorance that the first skandha has played on you.

So shamatha meditation practice is very important. It is the key practice for further development through all the yanas of Buddhism.

STUDENT: Is the experience of boredom also an experience of egolessness?

TRUNGPA RINPOCHE: It is an experience of egolessness rather than an egoless state.

S: The ego is experiencing the boredom?

TR: Yes, ego is experiencing its own hollowness. This is still experience, not achievement. If there is achievement, you don't experience egolessness, but this is the experience of egolessness.

STUDENT: Doesn't the boredom just become another form of entertainment?

TRUNGPA RINPOCHE: I don't think so. It's too straightforward, too frustrating to be entertaining. I mean the idea of it might be entertaining now, but when you are actually experiencing it . . .

S: Well, you were talking about pain being entertaining.

TR: That's different. In pain, something's happening; in boredom, nothing's happening.

STUDENT: Sometimes I'm sitting meditating and I notice strange neurotic things happening to me. I try to understand them, but as soon as I try to understand, I just get confusion. Is it best to just drop it?

TRUNGPA RINPOCHE: You don't have to try to do anything with it, particularly. Just let it arise and fall away of its own accord. One of the important aspects of the proper attitude toward meditation is understanding that it is a very simple process that does not have any schemes in it. Of course sitting and breathing is a scheme to some extent, but in order to remove dirt we have to put soap on the body. So something has to be applied. You have put another kind of dirt on in order to remove the existing dirt. But it's not very much and it's the closest we can get to [no schemes at all].

STUDENT: What do you do with your emotions when they arise? What about anger, for example? Suppressing it just seems to be a cop-out.

TRUNGPA RINPOCHE: If, when you're angry, you just go out and have a fight with somebody, that's also a cop-out. That's another way of suppressing your anger. You can't handle it, therefore you try some other way. Whether you do that or suppress, you are not relating with your emotions completely. The real way of relating with an emotion is just to watch it arise, experience its crescendo, and then find out if that emotion is threatening you in any way. You can do that if you are willing to do that. Of course, you could say you didn't have time to do such a thing—before you knew it, you just exploded—but that's not quite true. If you are willing to do it, you can relate with your emotions.

Emotions are not regarded as something that you should throw away; they are regarded as very precious things that you can relate with. The final frustration of the ego is the emotions. It can't cope with itself, therefore it has to do something—become extremely jealous or extremely angry, or something like that. But one can really watch the emotion: instead of relating with the end result of the emotion, relate with the emotion itself.

S: Not watch what it does to the object of the emotion?

TR: Yes, that's right. You see, usually in talking about emotions, we completely misunderstand the whole thing. We just talk about the end results, which is also an expression of frustration that doesn't solve your problem. It doesn't release anything; it just creates further chain reactions.

STUDENT: Your emotion can be telling you things.

TRUNGPA RINPOCHE: Yes, but you don't listen to it. You are just hypnotized by the emotion—that's the problem. The emotion is telling *you* things. It is talking to you, but you are not talking to it. You just become something the emotion manipulates by remote control. You don't have access back to its headquarters. That's the problem, always. That's why emotion is so frustrating. It finally gets hold of us and controls us completely. We are reduced to just an animal. That is why we usually find emotions uncomfortable.

STUDENT: How do you relate to the energy of your emotions?

TRUNGPA RINPOCHE: You see, there are two ways of relating to energy. You build up energy and then you spend it, or you build up energy and regenerate it. The second way, if you relate to the qualities of the emotions completely, you are able to retain the inspiration of the emotions, but at the same time you see the neurosis [that occasioned them] as blindness. Particularly in the tantric teachings, emotions are not regarded as something to get rid of but as something necessary. Also in the bodhisattva path, emotions are regarded as necessary. They become the seeds of the bodhisattva's paramita practices.[3] Those practices are based on the chemistry of the different emotions and how they can be transformed into different things. In tantric practice, the emotions are transmuted into different inspirations. Emotions are the seed of compassion and wisdom. They are a way to attain enlightenment. So one wouldn't try to get rid of them; one would try to relate to them. That's the whole point.

STUDENT: You mentioned watching your emotions. Even at the time of the emotion's crescendo, there's still a very strong watcher. Is it like riding them or watching them from the outside?

TRUNGPA RINPOCHE: It is not so much a matter of looking at them from the outside. It's a matter of embracing them as something together with you. In other words, it's trying to build a bridge. There's a big gap [between you and the emotion], that's why the emotion becomes uncomfortable. There's a tremendous gap; the emotion becomes separate entertainment. It becomes a separate entity that is going to hit you back. You become small and the emotion becomes huge and begins to manipulate you.

S: The larger the gap, the more it's out of control?

TR: Well, the more frustrating it becomes, anyway, because you can't reach it, even though you are controlled by it. So the idea is to build a bridge, or take down the barrier between you and your emotion.

As long as you regard the problem as separate from you, there's no way of solving the problem, because you are actually contributing toward the separateness. Your enemy becomes more and more terrifying. The more you relate to it as an enemy, the more the enemy can do to you.

STUDENT: I feel that my experience of boredom is very close to panic, like it has panic on the borders or is the other side of panic.

TRUNGPA RINPOCHE: Yes, obviously boredom is panic in the sense of not having a sufficient supply of entertainment. That's why you panic, sure. But that sounds like a very good sign.

STUDENT: Rinpoche, how do you transform emotions?

TRUNGPA RINPOCHE: Transform? You don't do it, it happens. If you are willing to do it, it happens.

STUDENT: When you talk about relationship with emotions, does that mean attention looking at the meaning of the emotions?

TRUNGPA RINPOCHE: It seems to be some kind of feeling of putting out a sympathetic attitude toward the emotions as being yours.

S: Would you call that attention or awareness?

TR: I think you could call it awareness. When the texts describe this practice, they speak of the emotions being self-liberated. In fact there's no difference between you and the emotion, so the emotion is liberating itself. The sense of separateness is just illusion.

I think one of the biggest problems is that we are unable to develop compassion or a sympathetic attitude toward our projections, let alone toward things outside our projections—other people, other life situations. We can't even take a sympathetic attitude toward ourselves and our own projections, and that causes a lot of frustration and complications. That is the whole point we are trying to deal with here. The boredom of meditation demands your attention; in other words, the boredom becomes the sympathetic environment in relation to which you can develop compassion. [In that boredom] you have no choice but to relate directly to what is happening to you.

The Dawn of Mysticism

The hinayana approach, which we discussed in the previous two talks, is generally very factual. There is no room for mystical inspiration. It is very down to earth and very definite. In the third yana, the mahayana, which is also called the bodhisattva path, or path of the Buddhist warrior, some sense of a mysticism, just an element of it, begins to develop. Of course when we get to tantra, or the vajrayana, the mysticism becomes more obvious.

Let us discuss the meaning of mysticism from the Buddhist point of view. Here mysticism has more to do with the depth of the potentiality for enlightenment than with any sense of uncovering something mysterious. Mysticism is often associated with a mysterious secret doctrine. The relative truth cannot measure the absolute truth, and therefore the whole thing becomes mysterious. From a simple-minded, conventional point of view, mysticism is the search for magic, maybe not witchcraft or voodoo, but still magic in the sense that things will be changed from the ordinary way we perceive them. Another part of the conventional idea of mysticism is that ordinary human beings cannot achieve the heights of it, cannot create this highest work of art. Only a talented and highly skilled person is capable of that. This achievement is regarded as powerful and mind-boggling, like someone changing water into fire and going on to drink it and have it quench his thirst. These are the kinds of things we read about in the books about Don Juan. They are involved with the mystery of hidden forces and things like the magical transference of objects. We also read about that kind of thing in the stories of saints and great spiritual masters: water is changed into wine, Milarepa flies through the air, Padmasambhava causes earthquakes.[1] These kinds of ideas of powerful magic that mystics can develop are widely found in the mysticism of Christianity, Buddhism, Judaism, et cetera. Everybody looks forward with excitement to the possibility of becoming a superpractitioner, a complete adept of the practices, so that they can perform miracles. Wouldn't that be fun? There is such a sense of envy!

Scientists also look for proof of spirituality in the same terms. If there is such a thing as high spirituality, if there is a supreme achievement like enlightenment, someone who has accomplished that should be able to perform a miracle. That would be regarded as proof of their spiritual attainment. Scientists prefer to remain skeptical, scientifically objective, but at the same time they look for such proofs.

There is great excitement and a tremendous sense of confirmation associated with this kind of magic. One imagines students comparing notes as to which guru performs the most sophisticated kinds of miracles. But from the Buddhist point of view, mysticism is not concerned with this kind of magic. We might describe the mahayana as the dawn of mysticism and the vajrayana as the sunrise of mysticism. And naturally mysticism in the mahayana and the vajrayana does have to do with uncovering the unknown. But it is not a question of receiving training in order to perform magic in the sense just described.

There seem to be two different approaches to magic. We could say that the attainment of enlightenment is also magic. Working on ego, which is anti-enlightenment, produces enlightenment, which is extraordinarily magical. But this is not magic in the style of the cartoons, involving supermen and so on.

Mahayana is the dawn of mysticism because here we begin to get a hint that there is something more than the five skandhas that we experienced on the hinayana level. Different views of this were taken by the two main mahayana philosophical schools, the Yogachara and the Madhyamaka schools.

The Yogachara approach to the discovery that there is something more than the five skandhas focuses on the notion that there is a discoverer of the existence of ego. Did the ego discover itself? Did the ego discover its own deception, or is there something else [that made that discovery]? Ego did discover its own deception, but there is some kind of intelligence that enabled ego to see its own emptiness. Ego's perception of its own emptiness, ego cutting through ignorance, is not ego as such; it is intelligence. So at this point we have to be clear about the difference between ego and wisdom.

Ego is that which thrives on the security of your existence. Beyond that there is intelligence that sees the foolishness in trying to thrive on your security. It sees that insecurity is the ego's problem. The intelligence that sees that is called *tathagatagarbha* in Sanskrit, which means "buddha nature." Every act that perceives pain and impermanence and egolessness and the five skandhas, and even that which perceives meditation itself, is an act of non-ego. In other words, we could say that ego has two aspects: one is the honest and solid, sincere ego; the other is the critical surveyor of the whole situation, which is somewhat intelligent and more flexible and spacious. That aspect that is spacious and flexible, intelligent, is regarded as non-ego and called tathagatagarbha.

The first dawn of the bodhisattva path is based on a sense of the continuity of intelligence in spite of ego, of some intelligence functioning beyond the security level, an awakened state of mind. Still, however, this is called *garbha,* which means "essence" or "seed," something embryonic. Whenever there is a doubt, some uncertainty, whenever there is boredom, that is an expression of tathagatagarbha shining through in the form of a complaint.

That complaint is that ego's administration is no good. This is like having a revolutionary party criticizing the establishment. In this case the revolutionary approach is much more intelligent than that of the establishment. So it is trying to throw off the government, trying to find its holes, its shortcomings, its points of ignorance, and so forth.

The first step on the bodhisattva path, and the reason why mahayana exists at all, consists simply in seeing that the mechanism of the five skandhas and the mechanism of the three marks of existence are not quite enough—that there is something more. The bodhisattva's approach is like that of an underground or revolutionary movement that studies the ego and also the deception of ego in its fullest sense. The ego is not indispensable. Tathagatagarbha, buddha nature, is the starting point of the bodhisattva's inspiration. You could say in some sense that the bodhisattva path is based on hope, on the conviction that the enlightened state of mind exists and that there are techniques of all kinds [to attain it].

Then there is the Madhyamaka approach to the bodhisattva path, which says that tathagatagarbha, or buddha nature, does not need any encouragement, because it is self-existing. It calls for the act of a warrior rather than an act of hope or positive thinking. This is more advanced than the Yogachara.

Historically, the two schools, Yogachara and Madhyamaka, co-existed. The Yogachara influence of hope and positive thinking produced tremendous inspiration in China and Japan. Buddhist art has been highly influenced by the Yogachara school, because it is aesthetically positive and hopeful as well as philosophically positive and hopeful. The Yogachara was also a major influence on the practice of Zen. For instance, the [third] Chinese patriarch's [Seng-ts'an's] work, *On Trust in the Heart,* is the epitome of the Yogachara approach of negating everything, that is, of transcending dualistic comparison. This transcending is the hope, the promise, held out by the Yogacharins. Transcending a promise is a promise. Transcending the extremes of both good and bad produces ultimate goodness; it is a promise. But from another angle the Yogachara point of view is a slightly weak one, to speak euphemistically. In spite of transcending dualistic concepts of all kinds, it still speaks as though God's on your side, as it were. What it says is comparable to saying we transcend both God and the devil and that that very transcendence is a noble action, an action toward the highest, the ultimate goodness.

There are some problems in that. What I want to get across here is that, to begin with, the bodhisattva's approach, the mahayana approach, is a very positive and very hopeful one. It is also very profound. The discovery of buddha nature is a very profound and accurate one. But when we make a big deal out of buddha nature as a promise, there is a possibility of falling into eternalism.[2] There is a possibility of going against the transitoriness of life and experiences, of going against the original discoveries of the hinayana level. In the hinayana level, we discovered that everything is impermanent, and now we are looking for hope.

The Madhyamaka, which is the highest philosophical approach ever developed in Buddhism, cuts the hope. Instead of being hopeful, you develop another attitude, which is that of the warrior. If a warrior lives within hope, that makes him a very weak warrior. He is still concerned with his success. If the warrior no longer has the hope of achieving success, he has nothing to lose. Therefore enemies find it very difficult to attack him. The warrior will also regard a defeat as a victory, since he has nothing to lose.

This approach is called "luring an enemy into your territory." You lure enemies into your territory by giving in to defeat constantly. The enemies finally find that there is nothing to attack, and they feel they have been fooled. They keep on conquering more territory, but their opponent places no value on the territory and does not put up a struggle. This eventually causes the enemies to lose heart.

At the same time, however, it seems to be necessary to have some kind of hope. We seem to need some positive thinking. In this case that thinking is that there is a definite, very solid basic mind that provides the basis for the warrior mentality. There is something more than ignorance, something more than just the big joke that ego has created. The bodhisattva path is characterized by great vision, great action, and great realization. The great vision here is the hope or positive thinking that the bodhisattva warrior does not need any further reinforcement or confirmation. You are already awake. So when you take the bodhisattva vow to devote your life to liberating all sentient beings, you also renounce your own liberation.[3] The idea is that in some sense the warrior has already achieved his goal. The very existence of the warrior has already defeated the enemy.

The warrior has no dreams of becoming a king. Being a warrior is both the path and the goal at the same time. Psychologically, the warrior's conviction transcends ego: there is nothing to lose and nothing to gain; therefore the petty games that ego plays do not apply anymore at all. This notion of a warrior is one of the basic themes of the mahayana. The scriptures often compare the bodhisattva to an athlete who has the highest physical training. The bodhisattva can regain his balance if he slips through the very process of slipping, so he never falls. The slipping itself becomes a way for him to gain strength. It becomes just another exercise for him.

The main practice of the bodhisattva is the six paramitas, or transcendent actions.[4] These are generosity, discipline, patience, energy, meditation, and knowledge. Generosity is the starting point. The reason it is the starting point is that if you think you are a warrior, you could become very self-contained and uptight. If you think you have nothing to lose and nothing to gain, you could in fact become very obnoxious. Generosity is a way of softening the bodhisattva's warriorlike quality, of preventing him from indulging in the warrior mentality. This is an important point.

Generosity here is not the conventional notion of being charitable. The idea is giving without demanding anything in return. You are willing to receive people into your territory, to offer hospitality and appreciate their existence and their presence—and then make no further demands. It could be very irritating and even terrifying to be a bodhisattva's guest because of his way of being generous. You might think there is something fishy behind it: "Why should this guy be extremely kind and friendly to me and not demand anything? Maybe it's a Mafia plot or something." But if you come across such a thing, you should not be afraid. Usually one finds a genuine act of generosity more terrifying than partial generosity, because there is nothing to hang on to. If it is partial generosity, we can play games with it. We could give half an inch in exchange for the other person's half an inch—it becomes a kind of bartering. But that element is absent here.

The next practice of the bodhisattva is discipline. This is self-existing discipline, discipline that need not be contrived or manufactured. It is something very spontaneous, a totality, total awareness, completeness. Situations demand discipline and you work with those situations. Discipline in this case is really more like fundamental awareness of things, of challenges in situations. Nothing is regarded as a temptation. Temptation is self-presenting, therefore you work with the temptation rather than becoming the victim of it or the villain of it. There's no pick and choose; the very existence of temptation is a reminder.

If you had a person with this kind of discipline as a guest, it might be hard to relate with him. He just sits there and acknowledges your hospitality, but nothing happens. The discipline of a bodhisattva in relating with hospitality or any kind of luxury is to accept the whole thing fully and completely. He also gets more satisfaction out of it than you would, because there is no impulsiveness involved. He is very straightforward, very close, very human. There is no flattering, but he takes advantage of your hospitality fully and completely, and he likes it. He eats your food and drinks your wine and likes them, but there is no frivolity. Sometimes it's so smooth that it seems too good to be true, but the ruggedness of the bodhisattva's human quality prevents him from being oversmooth, like a con man.

Patience is the next bodhisattva action—patience or forbearance, a quality of bearing discomfort. However, the fact that a bodhisattva is very forbearing in relating with discomfort does not mean that he has a higher pain threshold or a thick skin. This has nothing to do with his biological makeup—the bodhisattva does experience irritations. That is the most interesting thing about the bodhisattva's patience—he is extremely sensitive to all kinds of irritations. His intelligence is so enormous that he experiences *all* the irritations and sees all kinds of possible things wrong, as well as everything that is not in accordance with his or her taste. All the expressions of chaos and all the problems around a bodhisattva are acknowledged and seen. He is supersensitive and very efficient, but he does not regard the things going on around him as a personal threat, as we so often do. Even if something has nothing to do with us, we may regard it as a personal threat. Air pollution or rush-hour traffic is something that generally happens in a city, but everybody individually takes it as a personal threat or insult. Let alone the personal relationships that go on in our lives! They are of course a personal problem, but we take them as more than that—as a personal threat! If we were able to experience all the sensitive areas where things do not go in accordance with our expectations, we would become complete nut cases. We would relate to everything as a personal threat. But strangely enough, the bodhisattva manages to stay sane in spite of his higher perceptions [his greater sensitivity].

By the way, what I am describing to you are the practices of a bodhisattva rather than a myth that is being retold. I'm not describing a superman. These are practices we can do ourselves.

Patience is very interesting. Usually when we talk about patience, we have in mind someone who doesn't react to some problem or does not even see the problem, because he is *above* the problem. We think of an unperturbed person who is above all the nitty-gritty and hassles, someone who is raised above all that. We think of somebody like a nun or a jellyfish. If you had such a person in your car, that person would sit beautifully and quietly in the back seat or at the wheel, and if there was a traffic jam, he would still be grinning with enjoyment, not noticing the traffic jam. Then when the cars started to move again, he would go along happily.

This kind of approach is superficial. We have to think twice [rather than go for a simple-minded approach like that]. The bodhisattva is highly aware of the air pollution or the traffic jam or other problems going on in the world that could cause a mental freak-out. But he regards these as facts of life. He is not being philosophical particularly, not just philosophizing the whole thing. He also does not shield himself with a sense of humor, as if to say the whole thing is a big joke. Everything for him is very direct and human. At the same time, he is unmoved by these problems. Being unmoved involves intelligence as well as tremendous space within the intelligence. Intelligence is no longer conditioned by speed. When there is no speed in intelligence, it becomes factual understanding, almost photographic memory, so to speak, of every detail. Nevertheless there is room to relate to things, room to appreciate them. Also, there is no point in screaming if you're caught in a traffic jam. Bodhisattvas are very reasonable: if you scream and freak out in your car, you may cause another traffic jam. He knows that. He's very patient because he knows about the whole thing. And as a result of his patience, the bodhisattva is not a nuisance to society. In fact, he is a sane, good citizen. He is highly reasonable and wise and intelligent, and at the same time, irritable as well.

Then we have energy. This is not really a good translation. We don't have a good one for this. The Sanskrit is *virya,* which literally means "working hard" rather than purely "energy." Energy seems to be the product of the hard work of egolessness. "Vigor" might be better.[5] It is taking delight in your life situation of a bodhisattva and working hard. If we enjoy doing something, then we usually work hard. For the bodhisattva, every event is great fun, workable, wonderful. Not that the bodhisattva is on a love-and-light trip and so everything is wonderful, beautiful, and sweet. Rather, at all times everything is workable. At all times whatever happens is a learning situation that can be related with. This is possible because you relate to your knowledge as part of you rather than as information coming to you from the outside, as from some other culture or approach, or as part of some other style. Whatever you perceive—information, ideas, challenges—whatever you encounter is a learning situation, a workable situation, a highly workable situation. So there is a tremendous feeling of being human, of things being very personal. This is nothing pious, nothing philosophical as such. It is very direct. The whole point here seems to be that there is no speed involved in how you deal with your life, therefore you can't be bombarded with demands. Usually the problem is not that we are bombarded with demands; the problem is that we're speeding so much that we think we are being bombarded by things. In fact we are bombarding ourselves, and there's no room for movement or intelligence or breathing.

The next bodhisattva action is meditation. In this case, meditation is almost, we could say, aesthetic appreciation. This means awareness of body, awareness of colors, awareness of things around you, awareness of people's different styles. There's always room for everything that comes up. Everything is treated reverently, respectfully. Nothing is regarded as rubbish. Even the garbage heap is a work of art. Things have their own place, and you appreciate this, which is meditation in the broader sense. Both the relevant and the irrelevant are respected, so you don't have to economize on your time and energy. Because of that, everything becomes an object of meditation, of greater awareness, panoramic awareness. You take tremendous interest in different styles, people's different approaches, and the different physical situations of objects around you, and the different emotional states within yourself. For the bodhisattva, the whole thing is constantly meaningful and workable.

Aesthetic appreciation does not mean looking for beauty alone. It means looking at things with space around them. When things are seen with space around them, they have their own pictorial quality, so to speak. Things are seen in perspective rather than as representing demands or expectations. So bodhisattvas make a wonderful audience for the theater of life and death. This is meditation. But at the same time, the bodhisattva takes part in this theater, so the whole thing does not become merely a matter of impersonal observation.

The last of the bodhisattva's six actions is prajna, or knowledge, which is a governing element in relation to all the paramitas, all the transcendent actions of the bodhisattva. In this case prajna is clear perception. Generosity, discipline, patience, energy, and meditation each have their own precise intelligence, their own clarity. That element of precision and clarity that exists within the other five paramitas is the merit of prajna. Prajna is referred to as that which is able to perceive the unbiased nature of the world, which is seeing it in its nonduality. Objects of mind are not seen as mind's trip but are seen in their own right. An object is seen as what it is rather than what it might be or what it hopefully ought to be. Prajna perceives the shunyata experience of nonduality. That is perceived with the eyes and precision of prajna.

So we could say that the precision that exists in the six transcendent actions is transcendent knowledge, prajna, and the relationship to details involved in these actions can be regarded as the bodhisattva's skillful means. So all the bodhisattva's actions are an expression of the indivisibility of skillful means and knowledge.

STUDENT: Since you say the bodhisattva has already achieved his goal, it seems there is no evolution on the bodhisattva path. When you take the vow, it seems you are announcing that you can accomplish all the bodhisattva actions already. So how can you take that vow without being an instant pious fraud?

TRUNGPA RINPOCHE: It seems that you have to make some statement that sets up a landmark for you, and that is taking the bodhisattva vow. But taking the vow does not necessarily mean congratulating yourself.

S: But it seems that when you take the vow, you're saying that you can already manage everything the bodhisattva is supposed to do.

TR: Not necessarily. It's not as magical as that.

S: I thought you implied that the bodhisattva path was not evolutionary.

TR: The evolution here is that in the hinayana you have realized the nuisance quality of life, and now you begin to realize the possibilities of life as well. At that point you have to be pushed into the Yogachara kind of positive thinking to begin with. So you take the bodhisattva vow. Then you have no choice. You commit yourself to looking ahead. As a result, though you may not think you will be a good warrior, you become one anyway. It's like being drafted into the army.

S: I thought the Madhyamaka point of view was that you don't hope for something in the future, you just assume it's there.

TR: Yes. And in order to do that, you need tremendous assurance that it is there already. So instead of relying on somebody to talk you into it, you just commit yourself and take the bodhisattva vow. Then you have no choice; you've been cornered. You begin to pull yourself out on your own then.

STUDENT: You said that the bodhisattva sees all situations as workable. How do you work with violence and aggression that is directed toward you? How would that be workable?

TRUNGPA RINPOCHE: There must be some reason for it to be happening. Nothing happens without any logic. Even if the roof falls on your head, there has to be some logic to it. You can't generalize, but somehow if you are realistically in tune with what is happening, without being uptight and overemotional, there is a way. But, you know, there is no general prescription. You have to improvise as you go along.

STUDENT: If the bodhisattva is devoted to all sentient beings and also notices everything that's irritating to him and goes against his taste—when you relate to everything so equally, how do you decide what to be involved in? How do you decide what to be devoted to?

TRUNGPA RINPOCHE: It's very simple logically what should be your priority. You see all kinds of things on different levels and scales, and you pick up what the priority is. That's prajna. Prajna is precisely what susses out that kind of thing.

STUDENT: Wouldn't the priority be the thing you're already in, whatever that is?

TRUNGPA RINPOCHE: Not necessarily. The thing you are in might already be taken care of.

STUDENT: I understand how you can have something called generosity that is giving with no thought of getting anything in return. But even if you don't get anything in return, just having this conception of generosity and knowing, "I'm a good generous person"—that is a return.

TRUNGPA RINPOCHE: The approach of generosity is just being giving, and there's appreciation of the process rather than watching yourself do it. That the whole point. The meditation of the fifth paramita cuts through that, so there's no watcher involved. You just appreciate things and just do them.

STUDENT: I was wondering how generosity would be different from anything else a bodhisattva would do.

TRUNGPA RINPOCHE: In fact the six categories of transcendent action are not six categories: this is one life action. You could be talking to somebody and there would be the expression of all six paramitas happening simultaneously. You could help an old lady across the street, and the expression of all six paramitas could be there as well.

STUDENT: What is the determining factor in whether a person is ready to take the bodhisattva vow?

TRUNGPA RINPOCHE: If you're inspired to put yourself into such an awkward situation.

S: Well, it seemed to me that it depended in some way on having successfully completed the hinayana. Does that inspiration depend on having completed the hinayana?

TR: Yes, I think that's necessary. That is why the hinayana comes first. First you have to cut through your spiritually materialistic attitude. Hinayana cuts things down completely, you know: spirituality in the hinayana consists of experiencing pain, impermanence, the lack of your ego, and all the ego's problems. That is very important before you get into anything more than that. You have to have completely understood those warnings. This does not necessarily mean actually being completely free from spiritual materialism, but at least you have to have had those questions transplanted into your heart. That in itself might even be spiritual materialism, but nobody can just start with a complete achievement. You cannot wait for a complete achievement before going on to the next step—that would take centuries. So one has to trust that one can do it.

STUDENT: Is that the point that you have described as taking a leap?

TRUNGPA RINPOCHE: Taking the bodhisattva vow?

S: Yes.

TR: Well, that is a kind of minileap before going into tantra.

STUDENT: How does the warrior resist temptation without giving birth to an even larger ego? It seems that when you try to discipline yourself, if in fact you succeed at it, the ego just gets larger.

TRUNGPA RINPOCHE: You don't try too hard to secure yourself. You don't try to act perfectly. When you try to look for perfection in transcending ego, too much accuracy creates more chaos. So the whole thing has to be somewhat freestyle, if we could use such an expression. Fundamentally, you have to be willing to be a fool. You are not ashamed to be a fool.

STUDENT: In describing the paramita of meditation, you mentioned an attitude of reverence and appreciation. Would that be an attitude to cultivate in our meditation, rather than simply watching, simply watching our thoughts and our breathing?

TRUNGPA RINPOCHE: And in the everyday situation as well, not in sitting practice alone. Whatever happens in your life situation you don't just dismiss as being ordinary and casual. Rather, everything has its own place, and there is a balance there already. You don't have to create a balance.

STUDENT: What selects the object of meditation?

TRUNGPA RINPOCHE: One doesn't select the objects of meditation. They come to you.

S: Always?

TR: Mmm-hmm.

S: The content comes to you?

TR: That's saying the same thing.

STUDENT: But I thought each person had his own particular version of the story.

TRUNGPA RINPOCHE: Sure, but there's no censor. There's no censorship. Things don't have to be purely dharmic. They come to you. *It* comes to you.

STUDENT: You say the breath is a crutch, meaning it's something that doesn't come to you, but you have to sort of grab onto *it*.,

TRUNGPA RINPOCHE: Yes. That's kind of first-grade level.

S: Don't we sort of make crutches out of everything?

TR: No. Usually one doesn't manufacture crutches, but crutches are given to one.

S: We don't manufacture other objects of meditation?

TR: I hope not. Well, what else can you meditate on? It seems the technique is so spare; there's just walking and breathing. The rest is just nothing—it comes to you. The technique should be very spare. There shouldn't be too many techniques. There should just be one or two techniques at the beginning.

STUDENT: I'm beginning to see that the nine yanas are stages it's possible to go through one after another. I'm so over my head already, I'm wondering what the practical value is of learning about nine yanas.

TRUNGPA RINPOCHE: It is so you can identify with the path and understand that it is not only a myth but something you can do yourself. And also, once you're told about it, there's no mystery. The whole map is at your disposal. You can buy it. You can have it.

S: So as I go along the path, I'll always be able to—

TR: To identify with it, sure. That's what's supposed to be happening. That's why they are called yanas, or vehicles. You can't have a vehicle without passengers. Or without a driver, for that matter.

STUDENT: Is that how the bedroom and the kitchen sink come together, in meditation?

TRUNGPA RINPOCHE: Precisely! That's good thinking! That's the marriage of skillful means and wisdom, the bedroom and the kitchen sink.

4

The Juncture between Sutra and Tantra

We discussed the transition from the hinayana level to the mahayana level in terms of the perception of reality involved. At this
point I would like to emphasize once again that egolessness, impermanence, and suffering are a prominent part of the path, an
important part of preparation for the mahayana. The basic idea of
the mahayana is to realize shunyata, emptiness, through the practice of the six paramitas. But at the same time we should not lose
our valuation of impermanence, egolessness, and suffering, which
remain definite and important.

Egolessness can be approached from all kinds of different angles.
Self is not applicable anymore, because you have realized selfless-
ness. From the student's point of view, what is experienced is the
irrelevance of the self. This leads to the basic practices of the
bodhisattva's way, which bring further realization of impermanence and the nonexistence of self. Ego is regarded as a collection
of stuff related with the five-skandha process, as we have said. It is
purely a collection and does not amount to anything else. Therefore those five stuffs or skandhas depend for their sense of existence
on relative reference points.

From the point of view of impermanence, anything that happens within that realm that depends on the existence of self is also subject to decay and death. Life is a constant process of death and decay. Life consists of a process containing birth, illness, old age, and death. Life contains fundamental bewilderment, in which you don't even recognize the bewilderment as it is anymore.

Today we are trying to understand the basic meaning of shunyata. The shunyata experience could develop as a sense of the basic emptiness of life and the basic suffering of life, and at the same time, as a sense of nondualistic wisdom, inspiration. I feel that it is extremely important before discussing tantra to realize the nature of the juncture between the tantra and the sutra teachings, which is what we are joining together at this point, to realize what is the continuity there and what is not.[1] It is very important to realize that.

Self, ego, tries to maintain itself and develop its territory. Should that be encouraged or discouraged? Should we try to maintain ourself or should we not? What would you say?

STUDENT: Who should?

TRUNGPA RINPOCHE: I beg your pardon?

S: Who should try to maintain itself?

TR: Who is he?

S: Should we? Who?

TR: Who is we or who?

S: Should we try to maintain ourselves? Who is we?

TR: I'm asking you.

S: I don't know.

TR: Who is that? Who is that?

[Silence]

TR: Did you say you don't know?

S: Well, I . . . I suppose who is that.

TR: Yes, but who isn't that?

S: Who isn't that?

TR: Moreover, what are you talking about?

[Laughter, then silence]

TR: Who are you?

S: I don't know.

TR: Why don't you? Why?

S: There's no way of answering the question.

TR: Why not?

S: Nothing works.

TR: Why should it work?

[Silence]

TR: It's not a matter of con-manship. Things don't have to work. Let's warm up. Why should it work? Who are you? Why should it work? Who are you? Why should it work?

S: It just stopped.

TR: Stopped?

S: The questioning.

TR: Where does it stop? Where? Where?

[Silence]

TR: How come it stopped there?

S: I guess you can't focus anymore. Other things start happening.

TR: Understand that. We all show that common symptom. So much is happening that we find the whole thing bewildering, are unable to focus on any one particular thing. The whole thing is bewildering, bewildered. Constantly. Bewildered constantly all over the place. So we are confused, bewildered. Subject to confusion. We are a victim of confusion. What shall we do? Shall we stay? Try to get some sleep? Get some food? Or shall we try to get out of it? If you try to get out of it, it means putting in a lot of energy. Trying to get out means creating some kind of scheme so that you *could* get out of this prison. Could we do that? couldn't we do that? How can we do that? Do you want to get out or do you want to stay in?

It's a very inviting, smooth nest. Like being a worm. You could regenerate your next generation. You could retain yourself constantly by being a worm. Or you could stick your neck out by being a crocodile. You could.

Something coming up there? [The Vidyadhara invites a question from the audience.]

STUDENT: When you ask how can we get out or whether we want to get out, maybe the thing to do is just be aware of the mess we're in.

TRUNGPA RINPOCHE: Aware of what?

S: Aware of confusion.

TR: How would you get out of that? How would you do it?

S: Why would you want to?

TR: Precisely, why should you want to? Why?

STUDENT: It's not secure.

TRUNGPA RINPOCHE: Yes, it's so secure.

S: It's *not* secure.

TR: Well, it seems to me it's secure, because the whole thing is set up for you. You can swim in your amniotic fluid, and—

S: Well, for a while.

TR: You have your placenta, and along with the placenta, beautiful swimming pools have been created.

S: Yeah, it's fine as long as it works.

TR: It seems to work as long as the mother eats enough food. I mean there's no point at which we have to come out of the womb. If we are happy, we could remain there eternally. If the mother eats appropriate food, we eat and we get to survive. Moreover, we get the fun of swimming around in the water, behind the placenta, inside the womb. We feel happy. Great!

STUDENT: But isn't that a problem?

TRUNGPA RINPOCHE: That is a problem, of course. But how do you see the problem? How could we maintain that situation? We could stay there. What prevents us from staying in our mother's womb? What prevents us? What triggers off our leaving?

STUDENT: At some point it's painful.

TRUNGPA RINPOCHE: You don't know, because you haven't been there yourself. You've forgotten the whole thing. When you're an infant, you have no idea of it. You have to purely guess. If the baby had a reference point of relating with an open situation as opposed to the claustrophobia of being in the womb, obviously the baby would want to come out. But the baby has forgotten the reference point. It has forgotten being pushed into the womb and developing as an embryonic being. It has no reference point, so where would you start? How would you relate with the whole thing? How would you?

STUDENT: Is there a choice?

TRUNGPA RINPOCHE: As far as the baby is concerned there's no choice. It is just so. That's the whole point. [For there to be a choice, there has to be a reference point that sets up alternatives.] So why would there be an alternative? There is no reference point, absolutely no reference point.

STUDENT: Did we create that alternative?

TRUNGPA RINPOCHE: I suppose so. But there is no reason for creating a reference point as far as the baby is concerned.

STUDENT: People make the reference points for the baby, don't they?

TRUNGPA RINPOCHE: What?

S: The parents or other people make the reference points for the baby. The baby doesn't have a choice.

TR: How? How?

S: By having selves. By having egos of their own. They make reference points for the baby, and the baby takes them on. He doesn't have any choice but to take them on.

TR: Yeah. That sounds interesting. Yeah. How do they do that?

STUDENT: Doctors say something about the cortex connecting up with the hypothalamus. There's a different brain structure when the baby's in the womb.

TRUNGPA RINPOCHE: Yes. How do we do that? As a mother—

STUDENT: You tell the child how to relate to the pain.

TRUNGPA RINPOCHE: Well, that's at a more developed stage. It has already related with the pain; that means it has already made its mind up. But before that? How do we work with the birth?

STUDENT: It's what you said about emotions being the result of our projections onto the outside. The mother has all of those, so she's already giving them to the baby from the moment the baby is conceived. Even if the baby has no thought, he's already got the mother's—

TRUNGPA RINPOCHE: That's true, it seems. That's how we come to the conclusion. Duality happens—through a demand to go from one extreme to the other extreme. Duality constantly happens, going from one extreme to the other extreme. Duality is not basically a set pattern, but it has its momentums [that move it] from one extreme to relate to the other extreme. It's not preprogrammed as such, but it is related with a reference point that creates [a movement from] one extreme to the other extreme. Which is a very important point.

STUDENT: There's no memory without duality?

TRUNGPA RINPOCHE: Yeah, there's no memory without duality. Yeah.

S: Then how could Padmasambhava say there is one mind with continuous memory? In Evans-Wentz's book *The Tibetan Book of the Great Liberation,* it's stated that your memories continue.

TR: That's primarily in reference to the vajra state: one memory, one mind. You have to attain a state of one mind before you do that. The baby has two minds, or three minds, in fact: mother, father, son.

STUDENT: What happens when you see everything as just continuous events?

TRUNGPA RINPOCHE: You begin to see it as continuity.

S: See what as continuity?

TR: What?

S: What's the continuity?

TR: Nothing.

S: What do you mean, nothing?

TR: Discontinuity.

S: Discontinuity?

TR: As continuity. You see, the whole point here seems to be to relate properly with egolessness. Before we embark upon our study of tantra, we have to realize a sense of egolessness—because of the ego. This is something that is continuous but is based on discontinuity. Thus the ego is subject to impermanence and the ego is also subject to pain, suffering. The three marks of existence—pain, egolessness, and impermanence—exist simultaneously.

Of course we should not forget the glorious bodhisattva path we have been discussing. People have tremendous insight connected with that, tremendous inspiration to dance on the bodhisattva path. Nevertheless they should be aware of the consequences of egolessness and pain and impermanence constantly happening at the same time, all the time. It's happening all the time. So some kind of awareness of the basic framework of Buddhism needs to be kept all the way through. This is necessary, extremely necessary.

Ego, self, is based on survival. And survival means being right on time, constantly on time. You live on time. Throughout death and rebirth, again and again, you survive with your time. And because time is such a prominent factor, it is a source of struggle and pain. The pain and time and survival are based on the same continuity. So life cannot exist without pain and impermanence and ego at the same time. It's extremely simple logic, kindergarten level.

STUDENT: Is this pain based on the idea of securing something—because we have to secure some kind of permanent situation, we're in pain? But there's nothing to secure, and understanding that is the security. I mean, there just is no security, but realizing that is some kind of security.

TRUNGPA RINPOCHE: And so forth. You begin to realize egolessness that way. But you have never stopped yourself or created a bank of memory or created anything basic and solid, because your ground is subject to continual change and pain. You have no ground *at all*. This seems to be very simple logic, which I hope everybody could understand.

STUDENT: Rinpoche, isn't there an urge toward insecurity as well? Some sort of need to be insecure?

TRUNGPA RINPOCHE: Yes. That's very simple. You use the same logic all over again. The logic is that death lives. It's the same thing. Death lives.

STUDENT: How does this all tie in with the baby in the womb?

TRUNGPA RINPOCHE: The baby in the womb has the same kind of insecurity. Insecurity constantly happening. Therefore processes happen at the same time, as you go along. Babies are regarded as innocent, but this is by no means the case. Things with the baby are already happening according to its karmic situation. There is a reason that it is *your* baby, the baby of certain parents, which is a condition, continuity.

STUDENT: What you're saying is that pain and the knowledge of transitoriness depend on ego. You're saying that they exist along with the hollowness of ego. Is that right? Something is generated out of the sense of pain—

TRUNGPA RINPOCHE: I don't follow your logic.

S: You're saying that there is pain and transitoriness and egolessness, and these are three facts. And I don't see whether there's any definite relationship between them. But I think the relationship between them is what you're trying to get across.

TR: The pain, impermanence, and suffering are linked. You have ego, but you don't have ego. That produces apprehension and pain. The reason why that apprehension developed altogether is that you didn't have a relationship with the time. The time was not sympathetic to you, toward your maintaining yourself anymore.

STUDENT: Is that why paranoia seems to increase as—

TRUNGPA RINPOCHE: Yes. To some extent you could say that you exist. You think you exist. And your goal exists. But then you find that the existence of your goal needs maintenance, and that maintenance is a painful thing to do, to the point where *your* existence becomes questionable at the same time.

I mean, it's very simple logic, extremely simple, first-grade level. You distinguish between A and B and C. If you get beyond that, you relate with D, E, and F. It's that simple. The reason why A is A is because B is something else, and C is something else again, because the B is not the A, and the C is not the B. Then you go on experimenting until you get to the X. None of the letters are the same as the previous ones. They each have different characteristics. And so forth.

Well, perhaps we should stop at this point. Tomorrow, hopefully, we will discuss tantra. But I haven't asked my boss yet.

Thank you.

5

Overcoming Moralism

We have discussed the hinayana level represented by the shravaka yana and the pratyekabuddha yana and the mahayana level, represented by the practice ideal of the bodhisattva. Last, we discussed the shunyata principle. At this point, instead of discussing the first tantric yana, the kriya yoga tantra, it might be helpful to give an introduction to tantra as a whole. We could get into the details of the six tantric yanas later on.

As has been indicated, the impermanence, suffering, and egolessness that we discover on the hinayana level play an extremely important part, a crucial part, in tantra as well. We cannot deny this. It is important to understand and acknowledge that we are not just transcending hinayana and latching on to the higher hopes of tantra. Likewise, we cannot ignore the bodhisattva's path, involving the transplantation of bodhichitta into one's mind and the practice of the six paramitas. [1] Also the bodhisattva's understanding of nonduality is quite important.

It seems that we do need these technical understandings in order to understand the buddhadharma. The idea of the buddhadharma is not particularly to make you into professors or scholars as such. Nevertheless, when we discuss big ideas, powerful ideas, those ideas have to have some specific elements to relate with. So

tantra is desperately dependent on an understanding of the hinayana and mahayana, always. Some little technical knowledge of
the hinayana principles concerning reality and the mahayana's
principles of morality is a basic necessity, absolutely important.
If you don't have any understanding of those, probably you will
miss the whole point of vajrayana, or tantra.

People in the West usually think that tantra is concerned purely
with pranayama, mudras, vizualizations, and so on.[2] They think
that's what tantra is all about, which is not quite true. There's
something more than that.

To begin with, tantra is based on the understanding of who is
practicing tantra. Who are we? Who am I? If you asked a tantric
practitioner, "Who are you?," he would automatically say, using
the same logic developed on the hinayana level, "I am a collection
of stuff that actually doesn't exist, the five skandhas." This is also
the hinayana answer and the mahayana answer. And if you asked
the tantric practitioner, "Why are you practicing this path?," he
would automatically say, "Because I have surrendered myself and
my work is dedicated to the benefit of all sentient beings." This is
a pragmatic combination of both the hinayana ("I've surrendered")
and the mahayana ("I've decided to dedicate my life to the benefit
of all sentient beings").

The question might be asked: "What is the basic need to go
beyond the hinayana and mahayana? Why don't we stay on in the
hinayana and perfect the hinayana? Or why don't we stay on in
the mahayana and perfect the mahayana? What's the point of
going beyond those into another area?" The mahayana practitioner
would say, "The perfection of the hinayana is the mahayana; I can't
help it." And the tantric practitioner would say, "The perfection
of the mahayana is the vajrayana; I can't help it."

One of the follies of the bodhisattva or mahayana path is that
there is still a good intention involved. No matter how much we
try to be detached from our good intention, we are still involved
with it. There is some sense of a paramita, of transcending, of

reaching the other shore. There is an element of goodness that rejects the sense of energy. Bodhisattvas claim to be the bravest and most powerful warriors of all. But the bodhisattva's trying to live up to his virtue becomes a hang-up, a problem. Still searching for warriorhood rather than being a warrior becomes a problem. As bodhisattvas, when we sit down to meditate, we're trying to become good meditators rather than being in the meditation.

There is no pronounced good intention involved in tantra. Nor for that matter a bad intention either, if you're concerned about that.

We need to say a bit more about the mahayana notion of shunyata, which is discussed in the *Prajnaparamita Sutra,* for example. *Shunya* means "empty," and ta means "-ness." Shunyata is removing the barrier, the screen, between subject and object. Shunyata, the absence of the screen, is, for the time being, very important, very powerful.

A hinayana school of Buddhist philosophy says that everything is made out of atoms and everything is conditioned by time. Therefore it is impermanent. This atomist philosophy has been challenged by saying that such logic is not necessary. We don't need deductive logic to prove our point. In order to see the transparency of the world, we do not have to reduce everything to dust [atoms] or moments [atoms of time] necessarily. To do so is in some sense believing in nothingness. It's believing that things don't exist because they're made out of atoms. So what? Still there is some materialism left over [in the belief that the atoms and the moments exist].

Another philosophical school, referred to as pluralists, believes that a mass is a collection, which proves the nonexistence of the mass. All of the elements of the mass are conditioned by time and space. Things don't exist because the elements depend on a mutual space. And so forth and so on. It gets very complicated to discuss the pluralists' and atomists' view of reality.[3]

The notion of shunyata cuts through the position of the atomists and pluralists naturally by saying that we don't have to reduce everything into dust. In order to demonstrate the nonexistence of a table, we don't have to grind it to dust and then show it: "Look, this is the remains of the table." We don't have to do that. There's something else involved. If you are saying the table doesn't exist because it wasn't a table, it was a collection of dust, then you are creating the idea [that something does exist there that isn't a table]. Then you still have a pattern of fixed belief. The table consists of a pile of dust, garbage.

The shunyata principle in the bodhisattva's philosophy does not bother to say that. It does not matter whether the table is supposed to be solid or made out of a collection of atoms. That way, you still end up with a table in some form or other no matter what your belief is. But the bodhisattva would say that your belief itself doesn't exist. The reason your belief doesn't exist is that it is *you* who believe. Who are you, anyway? You don't exist in any case. That removes the barrier.

I'm afraid this is a very crude example. Very crude, kindergarten level. But in any case, since you as a fixed, ongoing entity do not exist, the so-called table, as you named it, as you believed it, as you used it, does not exist. Your version of the table does not exist.

So then the question is, what does exist? The barrier exists, the filter [between subject and object] exists. The optical illusion, the eyeglasses you use, do exist—rather than the projection or the projector.

What the shunyata teaching does is tell you that you do not need to have a barrier to name things. You do not need to have an interpreter to tell you what things are named. [The message here is] the nonexistence of the interpreter. Or the folly of the interpreter. [Without the interpreter, you have] no problem with language. You could have a relationship with language, in fact. Just kick out the interpreter—then you don't speak any language. That's fine. Then you are really relating with exploring things as they are. The interpreter doesn't tell you how things are.

So we come up with a very simple, simple-minded conclusion. Kick out the interpreter, then begin to explore. If nobody explains to you what a table is or what its function is, then you begin to explore its tableness—or potness or rockness or flowerness. You begin to explore, to work with things as they are.

That is what is being talked about in *The Heart Sutra* when it says, "Emptiness is also form."[4] Form is no different from emptiness—things do exist in their own right without your judgments, preconceptions, and so forth. [When we drop those,] we begin to see in a very direct way, a straightforward, literal way. The colors are not called red, white, blue, but they are as they are. If we don't name them, conceptualize them, they become much redder, bluer, and whiter, and so forth. That seems to be the idea of the shunyata principle: seeing things as they are.

But there is the problem of the possibility that when you don't use preconceptions about things as they are, when you reject the whole language and begin to explore the true nature of things, somehow or other you might be reduced to infanthood. You might become like a deaf person who never heard the language, though you still have a relationship with the things you explore. There's that problem.

That is the problem of nihilism. If you cut down the preconceptions so that there are no ideas, no fantasies, no categorizing, no pigeonholing, there is the possibility that you might end up as a deaf person, a stupid person. (This is a danger from the tantric point of view, by the way.) And there is also the danger [that of eternalism] that you might end up in an absolute, completed, perfected, meditative state in which you don't care what things are called. You are only relating to what things *are*. Both those are possibilities of raising the ape instinct again. There is that problem.[5]

Of course the whole thing sounds good and beautiful: you become completely detached from the whole world of preconceptions—there are no concepts, no naming; things are constantly organic, relational. That's a very intelligent thing. But at the same time, there's something that does not quite click, shall we say. Things do not quite work ideally in terms of how we function in the world, in the world of human beings. There is that problem with the mahayana way. The whole thing is moralistic. You try to be good, noncategorizing, all perfect—good and great and kind to everybody. You don't listen to bad language. You do still acknowledge bad language, but you don't actually listen to it. That seems to be one of the biggest problems with the mahayana approach to reality. That is the biggest problem.

That is precisely the reason why tantra is necessary. As you can see, you have to cut down dualistic trips of all kinds, conceptualized notions of all kinds, all kinds of believing this and that. You have to cut down that whole thing. But then we are left with numbness. And the tantric approach to life from this point of view is to redefine, regenerate the whole thing again: reintroduce duality, reintroduce conceptualization—but at an entirely different level.

You can't just begin as a tantric practitioner. That is not possible at all. You have to cut down your things. Everything. You have to cut it all down. You have to reduce yourself to numbness. This is absolutely necessary. Having done that, then you regain your perception. Another evolution begins to happen. That is the evolution of what is called energy or power in tantric language.

In the tantric language, we have the idea of *chandali*, which means "ever-present force" or "ever-present energy." That energy comes in reawakening from the sedations of the bodhisattva's trip. You awaken again, but still you have been cured of your dualistic problems. [You awaken to the notion that] duality is necessary. Samsara is necessary. In fact, tantric literature often talks about the sameness or indivisibility of samsara and nirvana. That means that some relationship is taking place that raises your intelligence after the devastating detachment, the devastating sweep, of mahayana. You have to regain energy from somewhere, which is from buddha nature.

So this reawakening fundamentally involves raising the principle of buddha nature, tathagatagarbha, as well as reintroducing the three marks of existence: suffering, impermanence, egolessness. But now they manifest in an entirely different light. Now suffering manifests as an adornment, energy; impermanence as a consort, to dance with; and egolessness as the basic strength to be. The whole thing is interpreted from an entirely different angle. But it is still in keeping with the understanding of life developed on the hinayana level.

Suffering is energy. Impermanence is a consort to dance with. And egolessness is a way to be. This becomes an extremely powerful tantric statement.

One of the founders of our lineage, Naropa, was a great student and scholar of the hinayana and mahayana. But he found that something was lacking in him. He had to give up his [monastic] robe and involve himself again with a teacher. He had to do all kinds of undesirable things that his teacher asked him to do. You can read about all that in Guenther's *Life and Teaching of Naropa*. You will find the details there. It's a very good book to read; worth reading if you are interested in tantra. You can find out more there about the outrageousness of the teaching—that nirvana is identical with samsara. That's one of the phrases that tantric teachers used: *khorde yerme* in Tibetan. That's a very powerful statement.

Similarly we could say that the teaching of the three marks of existence is a very samsaric statement. Life is pain, miserable. Impermanence—it's obvious: people are dying, we are all dying, constantly. Egolessness means that we have no substance whatsoever to hang on to. These are samsaric statements, obviously—the portrait of samsara. But embodying them in vajrayanic language makes them extremely powerful, tremendously powerful.

If you read Guenther's book on Naropa, you will probably find those three described as the three gates of liberation—in one of his footnotes, I think. That would be worth looking up.[6]

The whole point here is that tantric philosophy—we call it

philosophy for lack of a better word—speaks the language of sam-sara. Tantra is the language of samsara—the redefined language of samsara. After one has gone through all the spiritual trips of the hinayana and the mahayana, tantra is coming to the world. But in a somewhat, we could say, reformed way. It is more intelligent than the samsara-samsara approach. The tantric approach is samsara plus samsara rather than purely samsara-samsara. It is super-samsara, very intelligent samsara.

That is why tantra has been looked down upon by a lot of the hinayana schools and certain mahayana schools. And even in the twentieth century we have scholars who look down on tantra as being samsaric.

Dr. Edward Conze, a noted Buddhist scholar, is highly resent-ful of the existence of tantra. He would like to make the mahayana the glorious peak of Buddhism, make that the highest idea we could connect with. But then he finds there is another pyramid rising above that, and he says, "Oh, those tantric people are just freaks who just want to make love and drink. It's purely samsara, no good." Which is quite right from his point of view.

It is like Nagarjuna at an early age.[7] When he was a young man, he was an impressive, handsome logician of a mahayana school. At that stage, he would have defended Buddhism from tantra. But as he grew older and more experienced and began to think about himself twice, he became a tantric *siddha*. And that's the process Naropa went through as well. Why didn't he just stay at Nalanda University, remain a scholar? He couldn't do it. When people get older and more mature and begin to think twice about life, they always come back to tantra. That's true. It always hap-pens that way. You may not call yourself a tantric practitioner as such, but you find yourself being one anyway.

The basic idea of tantra from this point of view is the sameness of samsara and nirvana. The samsaric experience with its chaos and problems is obviously neurosis. Neurotic problems should be related to with detachment and openness, from an entirely new angle.

Why should we be too polite to samsara or to nirvana? Why should we be too cultured, polite, and reasonable? Let us turn the world upside down! Let us! Let us see the spacious quality of the earth and the earthly quality of space. That's what we will see if we turn the world upside down. That is the tantric approach to life. Space is solid, earth is spacious. And by no means can you call this perverted, because there is no one to judge what is perverted and what is not. There's no reason. Who is the perverter? There's no one to watch. You just become either the earth or the space anyway. Nobody judges that. That is called crazy wisdom. There's no watcher to moderate, to gauge moral obligations of any kind. You are doing it yourself.

So I would like you to understand before we continue: the basic point in tantra at this point is a further approach to reality. Reality could be regarded as unreal, and unreality could be regarded as reality. That's the logic of tantra, fundamentally speaking. That's why samsara is regarded as nirvana and nirvana is regarded as samsara. And we do not have any obligation to stick to one doctrine or another. We are free from all dogma.

STUDENT: Is the metaphor "stopping the world" [used by Carlos Castaneda] a tantric term from your point of view?

TRUNGPA RINPOCHE: I don't think so. "Stopping the world" sounds too idealistic. Tantra creates more worlds. You have hundreds of millions of deities happening.

STUDENT: Some time ago, when people used to ask you about LSD and other drugs, you described the drug experience as supersamsara. I feel confused, because at that time you used the term in a negative sense, and now you're using it in a positive sense.

TRUNGPA RINPOCHE: That's very interesting. It is precisely a tantric statement in either case. When you think something is supersamsara, it is turned upside down and made supernirvana. When you think of something as supernirvana, it is turned upside down and made into supersamsara. LSD and other hallucinogenic drugs could be regarded as an adolescent level of nirvana. Therefore, it is supersamsara. I still maintain that. People speak about all kinds of inspirations they have gotten out of those experiences. They think it's nirvana, but it's still a little samsaric version of supersamsara.

STUDENT: Could you describe how a student's relation to his teacher is affected by these various stages on the path. What is the importance of the teacher at different points?

TRUNGPA RINPOCHE: That is very important at any point. You need someone who will perform operations on you and will guide you and challenge you—a physical guru who lives on this planet. And speaks your language, preferably. And behaves like you, preferably. Someone like that is necessary, absolutely necessary at all points. There's no doubt that you would try to get away into your imagination of a cosmic guru. You can't do that. You need guidance all the time. Even if you realize cosmic guruhood or achieve cosmic consciousness, you still need someone to bring those down to the level of "I do exist." The guru is absolutely necessary; there's no doubt about that.

STUDENT: Is the interpreter to be ignored or actively thrown out?

TRUNGPA RINPOCHE: Actively thrown out. If necessary, call the police.

S: Who throws the interpreter out?

TR: You. Who else?

STUDENT: Could you say something about children and shunyata?

TRUNGPA RINPOCHE: Children and shunyata? Children and shunyata? I don't know. Well, they have a potential for shunyata, but they already have their karmic debts developed within themselves, which we really can't do very much about.

People have lots of trips, thinking their children can be scared or manipulated into a good psychological state of being. There are a lot of ideas about that. But it seems that you can't do that. When the children have developed to at least eighteen years of age, at which point the parents are able to see what the child's basic psychological functioning is like, then you can work with it. But I don't think you can regard children as fundamentally innocent persons. That ignores their whole karmic debt. If you think you are born pure and get fucked up by your life as you grow, that also suggests you could commit suicide to cut off karmic debts. Why don't you stop your life, kill yourself? Then you will be free. That seems to be one of the problems with that point of view.

In any case, children have their own hidden neuroses. At least as I watch my own children, I see it happens that way. Children have their own style of neurosis, and when they get to a certain age, like eighteen or maybe thirteen, they begin to speak out their demands, make their demands in their own style, which could be quite different from the style of the parents. And then, if the parents are well versed in working with people other than their children, then at that point they could work with them, relate with their style, and teach them.

S: But it seems that when children look at a table, they have a very simple version of it.

TR: Yes, naturally, they do, they do. But that doesn't necessarily mean a pure version. It's just that they haven't grown up, they haven't seen the viciousness of the world very much; therefore their ideas may be very innocent. But by no means are they particularly pure. [Thinking] that would be a big problem. In that case, there would be no reincarnation.

I suspect that all kinds of dangerous things may be coming up in my children. [Those things] haven't woken up, you know, but later they're going to come out. There may be Rudrahood of all kinds that hasn't come out so far. But we do not know.

STUDENT: Rinpoche, you talked about the attitude toward suffering in the hinayana, and then that complete sort of flip that's done in tantra with regard to suffering—taking it as energy or food. But I'm not clear what the mahayana relationship to suffering is.

TRUNGPA RINPOCHE: The mahayana relates to suffering just as a working base. It's a question of discipline. Whenever you feel pain, you are supposed to work harder. It's like when your tire gets a puncture, you have to work harder—fix the tire—to keep driving along.

STUDENT: According to the theory of dependent origination, when there is cessation of desire and attachment, you also have cessation of karma, of the life-and-death cycle. How does that relate to tantric philosophy?

TRUNGPA RINPOCHE: I think it's the same thing. If you transmute karmic relational action into energy rather than dualistic fixation, it becomes energy rather than karmic debts. It's a matter of attitude, a matter of having a sense of confidence that those neurotic hang-ups are meaningless and you have to transmute them.

STUDENT: Are they still there, though?

TRUNGPA RINPOCHE: The energy is there, but the neurosis is not there. That's the difference.

STUDENT: Is it possible to deal with emotions using that principle? And if so, how do you develop enough detachment to do that?

TRUNGPA RINPOCHE: Detachment, did you say? I don't see why you would become detached, particularly. In fact, you would be more loving toward your energy and emotions. They're a working situation, a workable situation, in any case. And if you begin to realize they are workable situations, then they begin to give *you* some kind of guidelines as well. The whole thing becomes a mutual project, rather than you just trying to get something out of it, to win something else over [for yourself].

STUDENT: Could you say something more about working with the neurosis in emotions?

TRUNGPA RINPOCHE: Emotions *are* neurosis, as we said earlier, but they're not regarded as bad or good. You try to find the nature of the neurosis, of the emotions, rather than relate with the manifestations of them. Manifestations would be, say, killing somebody, making love to somebody, or throwing somebody out of your house.

S: You seem to say, follow it down to the root.

TR: The root, yes.

S: How do you do that?

TR: You just do it. When you ask how to do it, you are asking for sedatives or gloves or hammers or pliers. "How do I do that so that I don't have to get my hands greasy?" It's like you're saying, "I have to unscrew this thing on my car. Should I use gloves?" There's no how. You just do it. It's also a matter of trust in buddha nature, trust that you are going to pick up intelligent guidelines within yourself. If you have enough trust, you're going to do it. That's the whole point. Everybody is able to do anything. Everybody is able to act out of basic sanity, in an enlightened fashion, in any case. But nobody has trusted them to be able to do it. That's the problem. There's a lot of hypocrisy going on—self-destructive things happening—based on self-condemnation. People feel basically condemned. That's the problem. I'm sure we can do it. I've seen that people can do it. I did it myself.

STUDENT: What does the ever-present energy or force you were talking about have to do with crazy wisdom?

TRUNGPA RINPOCHE: Ever-present force is the basic field, the ground that crazy wisdom dances on. The wisdom is there, and crazy wisdom is the action of it. In tantric iconography we find pictures of the *shakta* and *shakti*, the principal figure and his consort. The consort activates the energy of the principal figure.

STUDENT: You said that the three marks of existence are used for inspiration in tantra. I was wondering whether the six paramitas of the bodhisattva are used to do a similar thing.

TRUNGPA RINPOCHE: Yes. We could discuss that as we discuss more about tantra. Yes, the virtuousness of the mahayana path, of the six paramitas, transforms into an entirely different area. They are no longer virtuous alone. They become crazy-wisdom expressions.

STUDENT: Does Zen practice have anything to do with tantra?

TRUNGPA RINPOCHE: Zen practice is a Yogachara meditative practice that developed in China and Japan. Beyond that, there is the Madhyamaka philosophy, which goes beyond the Zen tradition and Zen philosophy based on the Yogachara. But the craziness of the Zen tradition leads toward the Madhyamaka path. A lot of Zen masters have managed to get into that as well: for instance, when they did things like burning the image of the Buddha or tearing up their textbooks. Those actions are expressions of crazy wisdom. Strictly in the Madhyamaka style, however, rather than in the tantric style. So the Zen tradition brings crazy wisdom to the sutra teachings, the mahayana, rather than leading to tantra itself. You cannot say Zen is tantra. That's impossible. Zen is Zen, and tantra is tantra. You cannot say Zen is tantra, because there's never enough tantrum in it to begin with tantra.

STUDENT: In hinayana and mahayana, they talk about the middle way. Is tantra also on the middle way, or does it turn that upside down?

TRUNGPA RINPOCHE: Tantra is regarded as an extreme way rather than the middle way.

S: You talked about a kind of reverse.

TR: Yes, a reverse. Definitely so. In the Buddhist tradition, basically you have the sutra teaching, which consists of the hinayana and mahayana. And then there's the teaching of tantra in six yanas. Tantra is the reverse of everything that happened before, including the hinayana approach. Tantra believes in duality, whereas mahayana believes in nonduality, the middle way. Tantra believes in extreme paths. For instance, you have the four orders of tantra, which are the father tantra, the mother tantra, the neutral tantra, and the transcending tantra. Those are the aggression tantra, the passion tantra, the ignorance tantra, and the tantra transcending ignorance and aggression and putting all of them together. These are very gutsy, if I may say so. Very straightforward.

S: I have one more question. Before his enlightenment, Buddha was practicing asceticism, and he almost destroyed himself fasting. In its reverse asceticism, its extremism, does tantra have the danger of being self-destructive?

TR: Yes. Unless you proceed according to the whole three-yana principle and have gone through hinayana and mahayana beforehand. I have been saying that constantly, again and again. You cannot practice tantra unless you start from hinayana and mahayana. Unless you have gone through hinayana and mahayana, you can't get into tantra at all. Without that, tantra becomes like a spiritual atomic bomb.

STUDENT: How does tantra relate to the teachings of the Buddha as they've been passed down through sutras and so on? Can tantra actually be considered Buddhism? What is the connection between tantric philosophy and the teachings of the Buddha as they were presented?

TRUNGPA RINPOCHE: I think they are the highlight of it. The tantra is Buddha's teaching. Buddha as Shakyamuni was purely a physical manifestation. His speech and mind are represented in the two stages of tantra. Any expressions of crazy wisdom or basic sanity can be related with the Buddha's teaching. To begin with, they are not deceptive; and moreover, they are work-able. They are in accordance with all the yanas that Buddha pre-sented. As I said, if you become a good hinayanist, you become a good mahayanist. If you become a good mahayanist, you become a tantric practitioner. Following along with that logic, Buddha himself is a heruka or the dharmakaya principle.[8] There is the story about Buddha being invited to teach by King Indrabhuti. King Indrabhuti was having his bath on the rooftop of his palace. He saw some orange birds flying in the sky, and he asked his minister what they were. The minister said, "Those are not birds; they are Buddha and his disciples flying by [wearing their saffron-colored monastic robes]." And the king asked, "How can I invite them to my palace to teach me the truth?" And the wise minister said, "Just invite them, prepare a seat and food, and they will come." The king did so, and the Buddha came. The first request for teaching King Indrabhuti made was: "I cannot give up sensory pleasures, because I cannot give up my kingdom. I want you to teach me something that will enable me to transmute my plea-sures into wisdom." The Buddha responded, "That's fine. First I would like to kick out my orthodox disciples, the *arhats.*" So they were kicked out of the place where the Buddha was teaching. Then Buddha transformed himself into a heruka. He created the Guhyasamaja mandala and gave instructions for seven days on how to transmute basic ordinary energy, confused energy, into wisdom energy.[9] That seems to be the basic story of tantra. Buddha was not interested in just banning the whole thing [the energy of confusion], but in relating with that as well as he went on with his teaching.

STUDENT: Where does enlightenment come in? Is there a point at which it's said that you can't continue with such and such a yana unless you're enlightened? Is there a place for enlighten-ment in this?

TRUNGPA RINPOCHE: It depends on what you mean by en-lightenment. That changes as the yanas change.

S: Buddha speaks about the point at which the wick in the lamp burns out. That seems to be some kind of definition.

TR: If you think enlightenment is something secure, there's nothing. There's no wick, there's no burning, there's no lamp. If you think of enlightenment as something that continues like the flame in a lamp reestablishing its position again and again, constantly, as a spark of electricity, then there's always room for enlightenment. But it doesn't have to be nursed as too precious to let go. It comes and goes, comes and goes.

STUDENT: What was that word you used that you equated with ever-present energy?

TRUNGPA RINPOCHE: I don't remember.

STUDENT: Chandali.

TRUNGPA RINPOCHE: Chandali. Chandali is energy force. It literally means the consumer, that which consumes the universe.

S: It means the universe itself consuming itself?

TR: No. That which eats up the universe.

S: What does that?

TR: What doesn't?

S: Nothing. That's why I say it's the universe itself consuming itself.

TR: That's it, yeah. You got it. Gesundheit.

6

Introduction to Tantra

Onto the disk of the autumn moon, clear and pure, you transplant a seed syllable.[1] Cool blue rays of the seed syllable radiate immense, cooling compassion beyond the limits of space, which fulfill the needs and desires of sentient beings. They radiate basic warmth, so that the confusions of sentient beings may be clarified. Then, from the seed syllable you create a buddha, Mahavairochana, white in color, with the features of an aristocrat, with the appearance of an eight-year-old child: beautiful, innocent, and pure, with a powerful royal gaze. He is dressed in the royal robes of the Vedic age or the medieval Indian royal costume. He wears a golden crown inlaid with wish-fulfilling jewels. Half of his long dark hair is made into a topknot, and the other half floats over his shoulders and back. He is seated cross-legged on the lunar disk with his hands in the meditation mudra, holding a vajra in his hand that is carved from pure white crystal.

Now, what do we do with that?

The whole setting is uncomplicated, but at the same time immensely rich. There's a sense of dignity, and also a sense of infanthood, of purity. The whole image is irritatingly pure, irritatingly cool. At the same time, one feels good even to think about such a person. This is a symbolic image from the kriya yoga yana, the first tantric yana.

As I described Mahavairochana, his presence seemed real in our minds. Such a situation could exist. There could be such a royal prince of eight years of age sitting in a dignified way on the lunar disk. He was born from the seed syllable. The basic principle of the kriya yoga is purity, immaculateness. Now that the practitioner has discovered the transmutation of energy, has discovered all-pervading delight, the kriya yoga yana prescribes that there is no room for impurity, no room for darkness. The reason is that there is no doubt. Finally, at last, we have managed to actualize tathagatagarbha, buddha nature. We have managed to visualize, to actualize, to formulate a most immaculate, pure, clean, beautiful white, spotless principle. This is absolutely necessary from the point of view of the kriya yoga tantra, because the rugged, confused, unclean, impure elements of the samsaric struggle have gone a long way from us. At last we are able to associate with that which is pure, clean, perfect, absolutely immaculate.

Interestingly, the effect of this is that we do not have a chance to turn our visualization into pop art. Such a visualization is quite different than, for example, if we confiscated a street sign in Paris and brought it back to America and pasted it on our wall. It might say "Rue Royale" or something like that. There is something quite crude about that.

Therefore the first tantric introduction to any practice is majestic and fantastically precise and pure, clean, and artful as well. In some sense we could say that the kriya yoga tantra is the tantric equivalent of the Yogachara approach of artfulness. There is that appreciation of purity and cleanliness.

One of the problems that comes out when we try to introduce tantra is that even if we do accept samsara as a working basis, we regard it as pop art. The crudeness is the fun. This is true with regard to sexuality, aggression, or whatever tantric element we might want to talk about. The general attitude we find is that the tantric view of sex, the tantric view of aggression, or the tantric view of ignorance is acceptance of the crudeness as a big joke, good fun.

This is one of the basic points we should understand through the example of kriya yoga tantra. Tantra does not begin with the idea that we have to live with death and make the best of it. Tantra is a self-secret teaching; therefore the teachers of tantra are not all that desperate to con us with the idea that we have to take the mess of our confusion as something livable and workable. Tantra is not telling us to cover up our pile of shit and think of it as nice fresh earthy soil that we're sitting on. There seems to be a misunderstanding about tantra that it came into being out of desperation: we can't handle our fucked-upness or the shit we are in, and tantra enters as the saving grace. Shit becomes pictorial, artistic, pop art, and tantra at last formally and legally acknowledges that we should put up with it.

Such an approach simply presents another problem. If tantra is simply willing to put up with these problems—without seeing their purity and cleanness—then tantra would just be another depression. It would also be uncompassionate. Still, a lot of people hold this view about tantra. They think its function is to accept the crudeness and clumsiness logically and legally into the spiritual picture. Because of tantra, we can be crude and dirty. In fact, we could jump into tantra by being crude and dirty and taking pride in it. Then we could freak out with crazy wisdom, and so forth.

However, just as bodhisattvas or those traveling on the bodhisattva path are good citizens, tantric yogis are also good citizens, equally good citizens, extremely good citizens. They are by no means to be regarded as the freaks or hippies of society, if I may use such terms.

We also have a problem about visualization practice and formless meditation in tantra, which it might be a good idea to bring out here at the beginning of our discussion. Visualization, in tantra is not a matter of fantasizing about a form, image, or object. Also, the students have to have a clear idea about which tantric yana they are involved in, whether it is the kriya yoga yana, the upa yoga yana, the yoga yana, the mahayoga yana, or one of the others. There is a definite attitude and understanding appropriate to each one of these. The students' visualization practice has to undergo some growth, an evolutionary process [as they pass from one yana to the next].

Before we discuss the kriya yoga tantra approach to visualization, let me point out that the student of kriya yoga yana, needless to say, has to have acquired the hinayana understanding of suffering, impermanence, and egolessness from the shravaka yana level. Moreover, they must have some understanding of the structure of ego from the pratyekabuddha yana. The student of kriya yoga yana should also have an understanding of the shunyata principle and its application in the six paramita practices. By no means is the student expected to have reached perfection in any of those levels, but at least he should have had glimpses into all these things. He must have worked on those other stages of the path before he treads on the path of tantra. This is absolutely necessary.

One Nyingma teacher said that relating with tantric visualization practice is like going to bed with a pregnant tigress.[2] She might get hungry in the middle of the night and decide to eat you up. Or she might begin to nurse you and create a warm, furry space. The kriya yoga tantra text, the *Vajramala*, speaks of those who have mistaken views about visualization. Instead of attaining Vajrasattvahood,[3] for example, they attain Rudrahood, the highest attainment of egohood, they attain the level of the cosmic ape, the cosmic monster.

A lot of tantric scriptures warn us about the difference between a mistaken approach to visualization and complete, proper visualization. In the case of the mistaken approach, the visualizations are related to purely as mental objects—you create your own image out of wishful thinking. In the middle of your ordinary meditation practice, you might get sexual fantasies of all kinds and decide to go into all the details of these fantasies: stage one, stage two, fourth stage, fifth stage, trying to make the details as entertaining as possible. The same thing can happen in tantric visualizations. Even if you are visualizing a simple Mahavairochana, a child sitting on a lunar disk, you might have the same problem. You simply re-create your own mental image, which results in the end in the cosmic ape. You say, "I am Mahavairochana. I am one with him, therefore I could become him." You take the [defiant] approach of "I am what I am." There is a sense of the beast, of a powerful chest, the cosmic gorilla.

Visualization practice has to be inspired by a sense of hopelessness, or egolessness, which amounts to the same thing. You can't con yourself, let alone your friends. There is a sense of desperation about losing your territory. The carpet has been pulled out from under your feet. You are suspended in nowhere. You have an understanding of egolessness, impermanence, and so forth, as well as a sense of nonduality—the barrier between you and other doesn't exist. You need not have complete comprehension of this all the time, but if you have at least a glimpse of it, then you can flash your nonexistence, shunyata, egolessness, and then visualize. This is extremely important.

According to tradition, when the vajrayana teachings were brought to Tibet, to begin with there was great emphasis on the teaching of surrendering. The teacher Atisha Dipankara,[4] an Indian master who established Buddhist practices in Tibet, was known as the refuge teacher because he placed so much emphasis on surrendering, giving, opening, giving up holding on to something.[5]

Taking this point of view of surrendering, before we start visualization, we have to use up all our mental gossip, or at least take out a corner of it. This doesn't mean that we have to achieve a state of mind in which there is no mental gossip at all, but at least we have to be approaching it. The starting point for achieving this is *anapanasati*, as it is called in Pali, *smriti-upasthana* in Sanskrit, which is mindfulness of breathing. The development of mindfulness and awareness, *shi-ne* and *lhakthong* in Tibetan [*shamatha* and *vipashyana* in Sanskrit], and *trenpa nyewar jokpa*, are important.[6]

Without awareness of resting your heart, trenpa nyewar jokpa—
trenpa literally means "recollection" or "reflection"; *nyewar jokpa*
means "complete resting"—there's no way of beginning basic
tantric visualization practice at all.

Having those basic foundations makes it possible for a person
to realize why such emphasis is placed on purity and cleanness in
the kriya yoga tantra. The immaculate quality of the visualization
of Mahavairochana, born from a seed syllable and sitting on the
lunar disk, becomes more impressive, highly impressive. That
particular sambhogakaya buddha becomes so beautiful because
you are unbiased to begin with.[7] If something comes out of unbiasedness, then the whole thing becomes so expressive, so fantastic. It's double purity, or 100 percent purity, shall we say. This is
purity that never needed to be washed, bathed, cleaned. It never
needed to go through a washing machine.

If you try to apply Ajax to clean up your dirty image to a state
of purity, then you create a further mess. The purity of the tantric
view is fantastically real. The visualizer does not have to question,
"Am I imagining this, or is it really happening?" That question
doesn't apply anymore at all.

People who live in New York City have a very vivid and definite
recollection of yellow cabs or police cars. But it would be impossible to convey this to a Tibetan in Tibet who never had the experience of being in New York City. If you wanted a Tibetan to
visualize New York City, you would have to say, "New York City
goes like this. There are streets, there are skyscrapers, there are
yellow cabs. Visualize them. Imagine you are in that scene." You
could explain the minute details as much as you are able. You
could expound New-York-Cityness to an infinite level. Still, Tibetans would have difficulty visualizing it, actually having the
feeling of being in New York City. They would have tremendous
difficulties. At the same time, they would also feel that New York
City was some kind of mystery land. There would be a sense of
novelty.

Teaching Americans to visualize Mahavairochana is like teaching Tibetans to visualize New York City, because they have never gone through that experience at all. So you might ask how we do that. We do it precisely by going through the three major stages of Buddhist practice: hinayana, mahayana, and vajrayana, or tantra. There is the hinayana practice of trenpa nyewar jokpa, the practice of recollection; and there is the bodhisattva sense of shunyata and of warmth and compassion. Those have to be gone through. Then you can begin to realize the quality of purity and cleanness and immaculateness of Mahavairochana Buddha.

Visualization is one of the basic points. The reason why it is a basic point is that through it you identify yourself with certain herukas or sambhoghakaya buddhas. This brings the reassurance of vajra pride. Vajra pride is not just stupid pride; it is enlightened pride. You do have the potential to be one of those figures; you are one already. It is not so much that there is magic in the visualization; there is magic in your pride, or inspiration, if you prefer to call it that. You *are* Mahavairochana, absolutely immaculate and clean and pure. Therefore you are able to identify with your own purity rather than that of an external god who is pure and who comes into you as a separate entity, as a foreign element. You are reawakening yourself as your basic purity is awakened.

A basic point about tantra is that it is not regarded as myth or magic. Tantra is the highest evolutionary process there is, and its whole logic applies to every step that you go through. That is extremely important.

There is tremendous emphasis on visualization in the kriya yoga tantra and also tremendous emphasis on mudras, hand gestures of all kinds. Executing mudras is trying to compete with the buddhas, trying to become one, trying to behave like them. Not in fact trying, but thinking you are one of them.

Vajra pride in Tibetan is *lhayi ngagyal*. *Lha* means "god," *ngagyal* means "pride." The idea is to develop the pride of being a buddha. You are one in fact; there's no doubt about that.

It is a very important point at the beginning that you *are* the gods, you *are* the deities, you *are* the buddhas. There's no question about that. But before you develop this pride, there might be a problem. If you don't think you are one of them, then you probably will think, "I am supposed to think that I am a god, that I'm Mahavairochana Buddha—I am supposed to think in that way. This is my goal. This is the message they're giving me. Therefore I should try to pull myself up." An approach like that is regarded as cowardly or stupid. It's quite flat.

In order to develop vajra pride, one also has to realize the pain—the vajra pain, so to speak—that is involved. Samsaric pains, indestructible pains, are also involved. So that pride has some valid point to be proud of.

In kriya yoga tantra, a lot of emphasis is made on a sense of purity. Things are fundamentally immaculately pure, because there's no room for doubt. At the same time, from mahamudra's point of view, the phenomenal world is seen as completely colorful, precisely beautiful *as it is,* without any problems. Things are seen that way because you have already cut through your conceptualized notion of self, the projector, and the conceptualized notion of other, the projection. Therefore there's no reason you can't handle the situation. It is precisely clear as much as it possibly could be—*as it is.*

I suppose one of the fundamental points that we have to understand is that tantra is by no means pop art. It's very clean-cut, clear-cut. Tantric practitioners are also good citizens rather than agitators or hippies. Tantric practitioners are real citizens who know [what is happening]. They are the good mechanics in the garage, who know the infinite details of how machines function. They have a clean mind, a precise mind. Tantric practitioners are good artists who paint good pictures—they don't try to con you. Tantric practitioners are good lovers who don't try to take advantage of their partner's energy, emotion, but make love precisely in a clean-cut way. Tantric practitioners are good musicians who do not fool around banging here and there; they make music precisely, as it should be made. Tantric practitioners are artistic poets. Tantric practitioners are in the world, but in the world in a different way than just getting lots of help by being critical of others and being dirty oneself. That seems to be the problem with bohemian artists. They get away with their approach by criticizing other people's purity. They are dirty and rugged and they take pride in that. People have some kind of respect for them because their criticism of purity is so intense, people can't be bothered to challenge them. Or they leave no room for a challenge. So people [tend to be impressed] and they say, "What you say is good, okay. Come into our society. You seem to be a powerful guy. You are dirty enough, and we accept you. We take pride in your being dirty. Let's create a poster of you. Don't wash your face. Let's put it up with you 'as you are,' as they say. Let's put up that poster and take pride in it."

The approach to tantra seems to be entirely different from that. It's not sloppy, the way you might think. It is very pure, very clean, very definite, very precise, very well thought out.

And there's an introduction to tantra for you.

STUDENT: You talked about a type of intensity and purity that emerges out of unbiasedness, but the visualization you described seemed to have something cultural about it. When I heard your description, it was really nice, but I got a sense of a Tibetan or Buddhist ritual. Would such an image be able to arise spontaneously in an unbiased fashion in me if I'd never heard you describe it?

TRUNGPA RINPOCHE: You see, there is a tantric iconography that has already developed [so you don't have to generate it spontaneously]. And it should be easy for us to identify with the tantric figures, particularly the peaceful ones, because they originated in the Indo-European culture. They're neither particularly Indian nor particularly Western. They are in the classical style of the golden age of the Middle Eastern kingdoms, from which Western culture is also partly derived.

In any case, it is precisely the point that a pure and complete image is necessary. The idea is for you to visualize something that is pure and clean and complete to begin with, when you are introduced to tantra. Later on, you will encounter wrathful deities of all kinds, very gory things. But to begin with, you have to realize how pure you can be in your visualization, how complete, how absolutely complete—even if it means that the idea of purity has to be purified as well when you first begin to visualize. This purity is the ideal goal. The tantric tradition recommends the inspiration of ideal purity, clean and precise. Moreover, there should also be something like regal qualities. You're pure, clean, and majestic at the same time. That is why this is called vajrayana, the diamond vehicle, as opposed to the mahayana, which is just the big vehicle.

STUDENT: Do you think that the visualization is implanted by particular conceptions of Buddhism, or is it something that emerges on its own?

TRUNGPA RINPOCHE: I think it's cosmic. The features of the figure you visualize do not have to be Oriental; it does not have to have slitty eyes or anything like that, you know. There is just the idea of royalty. It is definitely necessary for you to associate yourself with a king. And in fact the vajrayana is sometimes known as the imperial yana.

STUDENT: It seems kind of like the figure of the samurai the way it is portrayed in the movies. The samurai always seems to appear in immaculately clean dress and is immaculately together with his situation.

TRUNGPA RINPOCHE: I think so, yes. It seems it's all right for him to be uncompassionate, but nevertheless he is clean and precise. The interesting thing about watching samurai films is the way they clean the blood from their swords. It's very beautiful. It is as though a work of art is being practiced rather than there is a bloody mess on the stairs that has to be gotten rid of.

STUDENT: What is the difference between vajra pride and the pride of Rudra?

TRUNGPA RINPOCHE: That seems to be quite basic. The pride of Rudra consists in trying to overpower the other. Vajra pride is identified with the pride of self rather than being worried about the consequences of the pride. There's no sense of conquest involved. Just being yourself is pride. In the case of Rudra, there is territory involved, as if you were a jealous king trying to conquer your territory. Whereas if you are a universal monarch already, you don't have to conquer your territory. Being yourself is being king, and you take pride in that.

S: Is vajra pride more than just an attitude, then?

TR: It's more than just an attitude, yes. It involves emotion and intuition as well. You feel you are the cosmic conqueror, and by logic you are, because there are no other worlds to compete with you. And by intuition, why not?

S: So it's something that will happen to us, rather than something we can create?

TR: Well, you can use the visualization as a means to feel that you are a king. All the sambhogakaya buddha visualizations are of kings. They always wear crowns and are dressed in royal costumes. You are trying to compete with a king. You *are* the king of the universe, in any case. There are no visualizations of subordinate figures; I can't imagine such a thing. All the visualizations of herukas are known as lords or kings.

STUDENT: That sounds quite dangerous.

TRUNGPA RINPOCHE: That's why it is said that wrong visualization will lead you to Rudrahood. Precisely. Yes, you could become an egomaniac. That's precisely why the whole thing is said to be very dangerous. If you do it wrong, you can become the cosmic ape king.

STUDENT: If it's so dangerous, requiring that you work through hinayana and mahayana before getting into tantra, why are we talking about it like this? Even in the lecture about egolessness, suffering, and impermanence, I didn't feel like I understood anything you were talking about. And then you talk about tantra and refer to it as a spiritual atomic bomb. I really don't understand why this seminar is taking this direction.

TRUNGPA RINPOCHE: That's a good question, an extremely good question. I'm glad you asked it. You see, it's like this: suppose I was kidnapped in Tibet and blindfolded and put on an airplane. When my blindfold was taken off, I found myself in Berkeley, California. Then I was told, "This is your world. You have to stay here. Work with your world, work with the people here as your friends." I would have no working basis. I would have no idea what America is, what Americans are. I'd be bewildered. I'd be completely, totally freaked out. Whereas if somebody approached me in Tibet and said, "You're going to go to America. This is the map of America. These are the mountains, these are the rivers. These are the cities: there's New York City, there's Boston, there's Chicago, there's L.A. And there's San Francisco. You're going to San Francisco, which is here. The population is so-and-so." In that case, if I took a plane here and landed at this airport, I would feel more able to relate with my environment.

S: So these ideas that you're throwing out are not so much the real study—

TR: I think it's a matter of getting the perspective and seeing the consequences of the practices. Our goal is to work with tantra. Eventually you're going to do that. But as far as the individual meditation practice of the group here is concerned, everybody is working purely on the hinayana level to begin with. But there are possibilities beyond that, so let us not make a militant vow that what we are doing is good [and we're not going to do anything else]. That seems to be one of the problems the Zen tradition is faced with. You sit and meditate—this is the only thing, and everybody becomes highly militant and fierce and aggressive about it, saying that there are no other directions and this is the only thing you have. If I may say so.

STUDENT: Rinpoche, don't we run the risk of not fully relating to any of the various stages? You know, we have one leg over here in hinayana and another leg over there in tantra—that sort of thing?

TRUNGPA RINPOCHE: I don't think so. In any case, we can see what happens as we go along.

STUDENT: It seems like this tantric approach is going to fill me with false pride and cause me to relate to something that's not real. How do I keep relating to the hinayana?

TRUNGPA RINPOCHE: Your pain in your life is real enough, so that will take care of you. Maybe we could say that your pain is on the hinayana level, and that will take care of you. But when your pain has developed to the vajrayana level, that will be another matter. We can discuss that later.

STUDENT: It's not clear to me how tantric visualization practice relates to the way you described tantra as coming back to the world, getting back into the energy of samsara.

TRUNGPA RINPOCHE: It's relating to your ambition to become a powerful king, a cosmic ruler. That is possible. At least you can become the ruler of a household. And tantric visualization is visualizing yourself as the ruler, the exalted one, a sambhogakaya buddha, wearing a crown, being powerful, holding a scepter. Which is coming back to samsara, with the inspiration of nirvana. The original [hinayana] idea was to abandon everything, be a beggar, own nothing. Shouldn't we visualize ourselves as beggars, wearing ragged clothes, eating no food, being hungry? Shouldn't we try to accomplish beggarhood? No, in tantra, it's just the opposite. You're rich, you're the universal monarch. You wear a crown, jewelry, you hold a scepter, and are the conqueror of the whole universe. From that point of view, you have come back to samsara.

S: But the practice itself of visualizing seems very unworldly. There is a big difference between visualizing and actually being a king, an absolute monarch.

TR: Visualization is the middle part of a sandwich. To begin with, you have formless meditation, and you end with formless meditation. In between the two, you have visualization happening. And this is also supposedly conditioned by the shunyata experience. So it is transformed samsara rather than samsara as neurosis.

STUDENT: You have sometimes spoken of meditation as a process that grows on its own, starting with the initial form of shamatha meditation. Are these visualizations a continuation of that in the sense that they develop on their own, or are there points where there is outside instruction from a teacher?

TRUNGPA RINPOCHE: As far as your basic formless meditation is concerned, that goes along through natural growth. Therefore you can afford to encompass visualization as well. But visualization is a new technique that is taught to you.

S: So it's something that comes from the outside, isn't it?

TR: Yes. It's similar to when your teacher says, "Go into retreat" or "Take a job" or "Get married."

STUDENT: When you are this pride in visualization, is that like in the *Heart Sutra* where it says, "Emptiness is emptiness?"

TRUNGPA RINPOCHE: Yes. Emptiness is emptiness, therefore it has form—in the image of the eight-year-old emperor.

STUDENT: Are these symbols of royalty—the crown and the scepter and so on—symbolic of taking responsibility toward beings?

TRUNGPA RINPOCHE: Yes. That is an extension of the bodhisattva's way. As a bodhisattva, you were going to take care of sentient beings. Now you are going to be the ruler of all sentient beings, because you are not discreet anymore. You know what you're doing. Now what you're doing is a greater responsibility—arranging a cosmic energy structure as though you are a king.

STUDENT: There is something I don't understand. You just said that your desire is to be the king. Earlier you said that you considered it cowardly and stupid to try to pull yourself up to be the gods. I don't see how those two things reconcile.

TRUNGPA RINPOCHE: That's the whole point. If you don't have the basic framework of shunyata and egoless practice of meditation, then it would be a pathetic gesture to try to appoint yourself king but not quite make it. Whereas if you have the basic training behind you connected with egolessness and awareness of suffering and impermanence, you don't even have to say it—you just become one.

STUDENT: There seems to be a cultural situation involved here. Having been brought up to see everything in terms of democracy or anarchy or even communism, I can't imagine a king being anything other than a high-paid crook. Being that is desirable in some way, but—

STUDENT: It strikes me that what we would like to be is president.

STUDENT: We can't see a king as something positive.

TRUNGPA RINPOCHE: That's a problem.

STUDENT: I don't see the point of being king. Why take on that position?

TRUNGPA RINPOCHE: What else would you suggest? Don't you want to have control of yourself, be king of yourself? That's it [that's what it amounts to]. You could visualize yourself as king of yourself. It doesn't have to be a king who is running a whole nation. You are the nation. You are the king. It's the same thing. Gesundheit.

STUDENT: Along the same lines, do you see tantric visualizations in America taking a different form than they did in Tibet?

TRUNGPA RINPOCHE: That has occurred to me, actually. But there is a big conflict about that among tantric masters. Very practically, should Americans be allowed to visualize seed syllables in Roman letters? Or should they memorize the Sanskrit or Tibetan? It is questionable, and I hope one day to sort that question out and put the whole thing on a real footing. That would seem to call for getting Shingon masters from Japan, Mongolian tantric masters, and Tibetans all to meet together. [They could discuss these questions and come to a definite conclusion.] Is there any magic in visualizing Sanskrit? The Tibetans didn't visualize in Sanskrit, but instead in Tibetan. At the time Buddhism was introduced into Tibet, Tibet was regarded as a land of savages. In fact it was called the land of the *pretas,* hungry ghosts, because Tibetans were so poor. They also were not as culturally rich as the Indians with their Brahmanistic culture. Still, they read the letters of the seed syllables in their Tibetan form. But certain practitioners would have a reaction against using Roman letters, because Tibetan calligraphy is more aesthetically appealing. They might think Roman letters look very flat, ordinary, silly. We have to work on those areas. I think that's our next project, to try and find a solution to these problems. Personally, I am more for nativizing—for making American tantra American tantra rather than imported tantra, as the Tibetans made tantra into Tibetan tantra. I'm all for it.

STUDENT: The only thing I can think of that is like the tantric approach in the Western tradition is alchemy. The visualizations are not just the same, but in alchemy there's the visualization of a king. There are visualizations of a whole pantheon of aspects of the self—kings, queens, the coming together of the brother and the sister. I don't see these as too different from the symbolism presented in tantra.

TRUNGPA RINPOCHE: Sure. Automatically the Western equivalent of tantra has been happening. There is another link of similarity: Christ is referred to as a king. The Christ principle is regarded as that of a conqueror or king. But what is the practical application for how Buddhist students should visualize and work with this symbolism? Should we visualize Mahavairochana in medieval Indian costume, or should we visualize him in medieval Western costume?

S: Alchemy would use a Roman king. You know, these are very powerful images. There is something in the West—

TR: I think there is. But you see the problem is that it gets more complicated when we begin to visualize wrathful deities with so many arms, so many eyes, so many heads. Western culture hasn't been outrageous enough to visualize a person with so many arms, so many eyes, who eats you up on the spot. The whole thing becomes so generous and kind, so cultured.

STUDENT: There are deities like that in Bosch and Brueghel.

TRUNGPA RINPOCHE: I hope so.

STUDENT: Rinpoche, could you explain how this kind of practice involving the conception of oneself as king of oneself relates to the bodhisattva's aim of working for the benefit of all sentient beings?

TRUNGPA RINPOCHE: It's going further with the same thing. The bodhisattva works for all sentient beings as a servant. Now that servant begins to take over and run the whole show as a revolutionary government, which is an entirely different twist. That's why there's a big gap between the bodhisattva path and tantra. A lot of people complain about that. Practitioners of the bodhisattva path really do not understand the implications of the power, the vajra power. I think I already mentioned Dr. Conze, who is in fact terrified by the idea of tantra, because of such principles as the king principle. How could such a king principle be introduced as a Buddhist idea, he wonders, because Buddhists are so kind and sociologically oriented. They are kind people who would never think of ruling a country. But that point of view is problematic.

STUDENT: You mentioned the other day that at some point, the guru is going to mess around with your life. Does that idea come from tantra?

TRUNGPA RINPOCHE: No, that's a mahayana idea. That's the saving grace. In fact, if you were a tantric logician trying to refute the mahayanists, you could pick up that point. You could say that the mahayana teacher also minds the student's business. Then that approach could be elevated to that of a ruler rather than just a nosy friend. That is one of the links that exist between the mahayana and the vajrayana. We should tell Dr. Conze about that.

STUDENT: Does one kill Rudra with a sword, or does one let him die a natural death?

TRUNGPA RINPOCHE: Both. By the sword *is* a natural death.

STUDENT: Do you see Castaneda's Don Juan as an expression of Western tantra?

TRUNGPA RINPOCHE: I see Don Juan as Western tantra on the Yogachara level.

STUDENT: Suzuki Roshi, who wrote *Zen Mind, Beginner's Mind,* says that any single method has its limitations, its techniques. He said if you do not realize the limitations of the particular method you are involved in, someday you're going to sink into a deep depression. The ground is going to fall out from underneath you. What do you see as the limitations of the tantric Buddhist viewpoint? And do you think there's another path that arrives at the same place as tantra?

TRUNGPA RINPOCHE: The tantric viewpoint is not one solid thing. It has six steps, six levels, ending up at the maha ati level, which looks down on the whole thing as being confused. Maha ati cannot be attacked or challenged, because it doesn't advocate anything or criticize anything. By being itself, it realizes that the lower yanas are simpleminded. After that, I think there's nothing. Tantra is not regarded as one block. There are several stages to tantra anyway.

STUDENT: That stage that you call ati, at the point where you're looking at everything as confused—you have a particular term for that, and you call that ati. You call it something because of the perspective you're looking at. That's a space. Now, obviously that space doesn't have a name. Do you think that you have to go through a Buddhist perspective, where you call various spaces various yanas, to arrive at that stage?

TRUNGPA RINPOCHE: Not necessarily. But if you transcend ati, then you are criticizing ati from a samsaric point of view, rather than seeing it with its own perspective of the highest enlightenment. You begin to regress. It is like you have climbed up to a ridge, and then you begin to slide down. That's for sure. Of course, there don't have to be doctrinal names or ideas.

7

The Five Buddha Families and Mahamudra

On the basis of our discussion of the kriya yoga yana, we can say that basically what is happening in the tantric approach at this point is trying to build a relationship between yourself and your projection. We are still working with the projection and the projector. A relationship between those two can come about because of the tremendous emphasis on precision in kriya yoga. That precision relates to our working base, which is the basic tendency to reshape the world according to our particular nature. The purity of the kriya yoga yana allows us a lot of space, a lot of room to explore the functioning of phenomena on the energy level.

The next yana is upa yoga yana, which means the yana of action or application. That has the sense of relating with our basic nature, our innate nature. The innate nature of different individuals can be described in terms of the five buddha families.

The kriya yoga is the first tantric yana, the introductory yoga yana, which clears the air and also provides the ground. It can be compared, in setting up a room, to first sweeping the floors and cleaning the walls—clearing out all the garbage. That's the starting point. Through this, tantric practice becomes real practice rather than a game, in the sense that the tantric practitioner becomes a good citizen, as we have described already.

Kriya yoga puts tremendous emphasis on purification, purification and visualization. Upa yoga, and particularly advanced upa yoga, puts a lot of emphasis on actual practice [in life situations], actual practice that leads to living a pure life. Upa yoga also brings in an element of crazy wisdom, which connects it with the next yana, yoga yana. So upa yoga yana is referred to as the yana of transition [between kriya and yoga yanas]. It is also often referred to as the neutral yana, neither masculine nor feminine.

At this point it would be good to discuss mahamudra, which is also connected with relating with our innate nature the way we do in the yoga practices of vajrayana. *Maha* means "great," and *mudra* means "symbol." So *mahamudra* means "great symbol." This is the basic core, or backbone, of all the [lower] tantric yoga practices. Kriya yoga yana, upa yoga yana, and yoga yana all involve practices that relate with the basic origin, *shi* in Tibetan, which also means "background." So they are yogas of the basic origin or yogas of the background, or yogas of basic nature. There is a difference between the higher yogas that we haven't discussed yet and these lower yogas, which work with the basic ground. The three yoga yanas of lower tantra still have some relationship with the mahayana practices, which also work with the basic potential. So there are a lot of references to relating with the origin, relating with the potential.

This is connected with mahayana's approach toward life, which emphasizes the potential of tathagatagarbha, the basic nature. Therefore your situation is workable. And it has been said that mahamudra, the great symbol, is also working on the basic origin, the basic potential. Thus the yogas of the lower tantra are also connected with something you can work with. You have a potential already. There's a seed already.

Mahamudra is a way of bringing together the notion of the immense emptiness of space, shunyata, and manifestation within shunyata. The shunyata principle is associated with nirvana and the manifestation of confusion that occurs around it is samsara. So mahamudra is concerned with how to bring about the indivisibility of samsara and nirvana. The samsaric messages of passion, aggression, and all kinds of things that we might experience in our life situation are not rejected but regarded as a workable part of our basic nature that we can relate with. Those are workable situations; but they are not just workable. They also contain messages that push us into situations in which we can work on ourselves. We are being pushed into that basic situation.

So mahamudra has to do with learning to work with the cosmic message, the basic message in our life situation, which is also teaching. We do not have to relate to teaching only in the religious context. We also have to read the symbolism connected with our life situation. What we live, where we live, how we live—all these living situations also have a basic message that we can read, that we can work with.

If you are speeding, you get a ticket. If you are driving too slow, you get a honk from behind. A red light means danger; a green light means go; an amber light means get ready to go or stop. If you try to cheat on your karmic debts, the tax authorities are going to get after you. There are numerous manifestations of all kinds. If you don't pay your telephone bill, the telephone will be disconnected. All those little things that you think are a hassle, that you think an organization or the authorities have created to belittle you, to make you public property—that's not true. There is always some kind of message constantly happening. In that sense, the existence of any regulations or rules or laws that exist in a country are manifestations of mahamudra. If you don't eat enough, you get hungry. If you don't eat enough because you don't have the money to pay for your food, because you didn't have the incentive to take a job, you are a reject of society. You can't be bothered with things; you can't get your trips together to go out and get a job so that you can have food and money to live.

We think all those little things are just a domestic hassle, but they also have tremendous messages behind them. Whether you are living in the twentieth-century automated world or living a rural, organic existence in Tibet, the hassles are the same thing. There is always something to hassle with, something to push you, pull you.

A lot of people leave this country because they can't be bothered with the taxation and money problems. They decide to go to India—that's the most obvious flow—because they think that in India nobody hassles you.[1] Nobody cares who is who and what is what, and there's no tax. At least, nobody talks about dollars. Instead, people talk about rupees, which is a refreshing name. Or they go to Europe, where people talk about pounds or francs, or whatever. But in vajrayana, you have to pay something. Even in an idealized vajrayana like vajrayana Disneyland, the vajrayana authorities still have to maintain that Disneyland. You have to pay something. You can't just get free hospitality. You can seek out hospitality, but still you have to be ingratiating to do that. Mutual hospitality is always important. When you begin to smile less, you have to pay more money. Even in vajrayana Disneyland, it depends on your reactions.

From this point of view, vajrayana means openness to the messages that are coming across to us. Acknowledging them, respecting them. Mahamudra also means that. There is a sense of appreciation of the basic buddha natures, that you are one of them, that you have a link to them.

Upa yoga yana relates enormously with both the practice and the inspiration coming to you from the situation at the same time. The practice is not as secure and clean and perfect as that of kriya yoga yana. In kriya there is the sense that if you keep yourself clean and safe, you will be saved. But not anymore. Now you actually have to work harder, you have to relate with reality much more than just within the limits of keeping clean and pure.

At this point, it might be necessary to discuss the five buddha principles. They are important in relation to both upa yoga yana and the other tantric yanas we will discuss later on. The five principles of buddha nature refer to the buddha qualities in all of us. We are not, as we might imagine, expected to be uniform and regimented, to be ideally enlightened and absolutely cool and kind and wise. The five buddha principles are the different expressions of basic sanity. There are five different ways to be sane.

The first is the buddha principle of the buddha family, which is basically being even, not reacting. Being steady, not reacting to excitement, being basically solid yet open at the same time. Basically sound and earthy, steady, but somewhat dull. Not particularly enterprising.

Then you have the vajra buddha family, which is extremely sharp, intellectual, analytical. You can relate with things precisely, and you can also see the disadvantages of various involvements. You can see the holes in things or the challenges that might occur. Precisely open and clear, analytically cool, cold, possibly unfriendly, but always on the dot. Seeing all the highlights of things as they are. Very precise, very direct, very sharp. Reactivity is very high. You are ready to jump, ready to pursue and criticize. You are ready to analyze what's wrong with situations and what's wrong with ideas. *Vajra* means "adamantine," which is like diamond, or superdiamond.

The next family is ratna, which means "jewel," "gem," "precious stone." *Mani* [Skt. "jewel"], as in OM MANI PADME HUM. It sounds close to "money." You are always making yourself at home with collections of all kinds of richness and wealth. All kinds. The world of velvet and satin and jewels. Magnetizing all kinds of food and wealth. Swimming through food and wealth. Richness. A person with the ratna mentality could be in the middle of the Gobi Desert and still manage to make himself rich and fantastically homey. He could entertain himself—the richness makes it so that all kinds of things happen. There is a sense of constant magnetizing. Those magnetic qualities make the person a comfortable bed, a nest. He draws everything in, richness of all kinds. That's why ratna is represented by a gem, a jewel, a precious stone. It's self-existing richness.

The next one is padma, which literally means "lotus," or we could say "blossom." Padma has to do with seduction, which is also magnetizing, but not in the sense of making yourself at home and collecting lots of rich materials like ratna. Padma's seduction is magnetizing more in order to relate with itself, maintain itself, prove its own existence. It is constantly magnetizing, drawing in, and making use of what it draws in. The idea of copulation is a somewhat good symbol—magnetizing and then making use of what you magnetize. Things are collected and made love to. The object of seduction is not regarded as a nest, but it is used—perhaps as food or clothes. There is a supermagnetic quality that is so great that the projections cannot help being attracted by it. It is very passionate.

The next buddha family principle is karma. Karma literally means "action" or "activity." Karma in this case is the action of fulfillment. Situations have to be fulfilled, so everything around you has to be efficient, speedy, functional all the time. If anything does not fit your scheme, you destroy it. So everything has to become pragmatic, functional, efficient. Things are collected because you would like to relate with the functionality of everything. Speed and efficiency of all kinds.

Those five principles of buddha nature, traditionally known as the buddha families, are the basic working basis that tantra has to offer.

In the tantric tradition there are different deities, different approaches to your action, that are related with those five styles. One of the important implications of this is that in tantra, everybody does not have to be uniform as in the bodhisattva's approach, where everything has to be kept cool and skillful, steady all the time. There, all the paramitas are good as long as you keep up with a certain central logic: you realize that you have buddha nature in you, so you can be generous, patient, and so forth. But tantra does not have this kind of one-track mind that we find in the bodhisattva's approach. In tantra, there are all kinds of variations you can get into, based on the five different perspectives. There are five different kinds of relationships with things, and you can identify yourself with all or one of these, or partially with any of them. You could have one leading aspect and a suggestion of something else. You might have a vajra quality along with a padma quality and maybe a touch of karma as well, and so forth. Basically, psychologically, vajrayana permits the openness to work on all kinds of elements that you have in you. You don't have to tune yourself into one particular basic thing. You can take pride in what you are, what you have, your basic nature. If your nature is made up of too much of the passionate element of padma, and too much of the efficiency of karma, those things are not regarded as hang-ups as such. Those things are regarded as basic qualities that you have.

I think that is the basic core understanding of tantra. Tantra permits different aspects of you to shine through, rather than your having to be channeled into one basic set of characteristics. It allows your basic nature to come through.

From upa yoga yana onward, into the other tantras we'll discuss later on, and in kriya as well, those buddha family principles allow you to work with mahamudra, the great symbol. They allow you to relate with the working basis of your lifestyle as such.

In the upa yoga yana, a framework of practice developed that is very much based on mudras and mantras. You visualize yourself as a Mahavairochana, and then you visualize a Mahavairochana sitting on a lunar disk in front of you. Then you send rays of light out both from the Mahavairochana visualized in front of you and from yourself and [with these light rays] invite the *jnana kaya*,[2] or wisdom body, of Mahavairochana—the true Mahavairochana as opposed to the visualized ones you have imagined. In fact you invite a host of Mahavairochanas sitting on lunar disks in clouds, along with all kinds of *devas* and *devatas*—goddesses, angels, cherubs—playing musical instruments. A rain of flowers falls toward you, music is playing, there are fluttering banners in the air, and songs of praise to Mahavairochana are heard. The wisdom body of Mahavairochana comes toward you; the little prince of eight years of age, the super eight-year-old, the higher wisdom body, descends and dissolves into the Mahavairochana you visualized in front of you. In turn you, as your imagination of Mahavairochana, however clumsy it might be, create out of your heart offering deities—goddesses, cherubs, angels—carrying food and musical instruments, who entertain the visualized Mahavairochana.

By this time the visualization in front of you has been united with the wisdom body. Now this becomes the authentic Mahavairochana in front of you. He is a real Mahavairochana principle, so you offer food, sing a song of praise, and so forth. All of this is accompanied by extremely complicated mudras, and mantras of all kinds. Then the Mahavairochana in front of you is satisfied with your entertainment and acknowledges the little attempt that you made with your visualizations, including the visualization of yourself as one of them, as a kind of immigrant to the Pure Land. You are accepted as a somewhat seemingly good citizen of Mahavairochana land. There is constant mantra practice and working on that situation. The visualized Mahavairochana in front of you comes toward you and dissolves into your body. That is the point where you develop your vajra pride. You identify with that Mahavairochana, you become one with it, completely one with it. Then you are crowned; there is a coronation ceremony in which all the buddhas of the universe come to you bringing jeweled crowns, which they place on your head. You are crowned as the Buddha, Mahavairochana himself—and so forth.

All those processes—acknowledgment of the higher imaginary buddha as yourself and the higher buddha who comes to you, and so forth—you could say are pure superstition. You have a higher god and that god is related with the imaginary god. You could also say that the imaginary god becomes god in you. Conventional mysticism would find that a highly workable description, extremely good, ideal. That is their idea of what you should try to work with: god is in you and you are the god, as Yogi Bhajan would say.[3]

But I'm afraid it's not as simple as that. You can't just say god is in you and you are the god, because god is not in you and you are not in the god. You have to make an effort. Those sambhogakaya buddha principles have to be invited, acknowledged, and then finally invited into your whole being. That is an entirely different situation.

It is entirely different from the child in the home visualizing Santa Claus at Christmastime. The divine Santa Claus approaches you with his reindeer and so forth. Then he dissolves into your father. In turn your father becomes the true Santa Claus, brings presents, and puts them in your stocking. The father—the divine Santa Claus—then drinks the milk and eats the cookies. It's not as folksy as that, I'm afraid. One could create an American tantra purely by using those images, but that becomes too cheap, a plastic world. Transplanting Mahavairochana [into oneself] is more deadly, more powerful. It is not on the level of a Christmas celebration, as though in the name of a divine Mahavairochana we would put a neon light outside our door. Or maybe we could make a cartoon film of it, or hang out a gigantic balloon in the air, saying "Mahavairochana is coming to town." One could try all kinds of things, but I don't think Mahavairochana would quite be amused. Nor would the lineage of gurus of the tantric tradition quite be amused.

There seems to be a need for serious commitment to the whole thing. Maybe I should stop talking at this point and let people ask questions about the whole thing. That might be more helpful. Is there anybody who would like to ask questions about the whole thing?

STUDENT: Are these visualizations actually things that come into you, or is it that you're visualizing in terms of art forms? In other words, is it just something you visualize, or are these situations that do happen because of that strategy?

TRUNGPA RINPOCHE: I think you could say it's both. There is inspiration connected with these visualizations, but at the same time there is a format of visualization that has occurred culturally. They coincide, they come together.

S: As to the cultural aspect of these art forms: are these the forms that the personages you visualize actually take? Do they take that cultural form, or are those just artistic expressions, drawings, representations, in which the colors and designs and textures just convey a taste of those personages?

TR: Yes, I think that's it. They are based on experience. Those figures have a crown, a skirt, a shawl, and ornaments, and that's all. They are not dressed in the [specific] imperial costume of China, nor in that of an Indian raja. They are very simple and straightforward. As far as Indo-European culture goes, they are very workable.

S: So they transcend culture in a sense, transcend Oriental culture.

TR: I think so, yes. The style is that of pre-Hindustan culture, before the Mongols invaded India. Those are just images that exist expressing the common idea of the Indo-European ideal of a king. So purely by chance, those visualizations are workable for us: a youthful king wearing a crown and a shawl, maybe a shirt with half sleeves—that's one of the iconographical forms—and lots of jewels, and a skirt. That's it. I don't think that this is particularly problematic. It's not particularly Oriental. In fact, it's highly Western. It is like Gandharan art, in which the Buddha's features are Western. Conveniently for us, this is Indo-European culture. I don't know what we'll do when Buddhism goes to Africa, which is maybe an entirely different area. But as far as Indian and European culture goes, there's no problem with that. There's no problem visualizing a king of this type. In fact, it's quite right.

STUDENT: What's the relationship between mahamudra and the mandala of the five buddha families?

TRUNGPA RINPOCHE: The five-buddha mandala is the expression of mahamudra. It is how mahamudra sees the world as the symbolic or real manifestation of sanity. It's the same thing, in fact. There's no difference at all. Mahamudra is the eye of wisdom that sees the five buddha principles as its vision.

STUDENT: Is the god coming into you a confirmation of the fact that you already exist as a god?

TRUNGPA RINPOCHE: Confirmation doesn't exist. You don't have to be confirmed. Because the confirmation "I'm the god and the god is me" doesn't exist, therefore the god doesn't exist and the watcher, which is you, doesn't exist. So there's no god and there's no you. As far as Buddhism is concerned, there's no god at all. That's 200 percent sure. There's no god. God doesn't exist in Buddhism. And ego doesn't exist in Buddhism either.

STUDENT: Who can be a guru?

TRUNGPA RINPOCHE: Anyone who can reflect you as a mirror does and with whom, at the same time, you have a relationship as a personal friend. If a person is too formal, he cannot be a guru. A very formal person might be all right as the legalized head of your order, like the Pope for the Catholics or the Dalai Lama for the Tibetans. Someone might say, "I belong to this Tibetan sect, therefore the Dalai Lama is my guru." But basically a guru is someone who cares about you and minds your business, who relates with your basic being.

S: Would one of the qualities of a guru be that he is a realized being?

TR: Definitely, yes. And also a lot of it depends on you, on whether you think your guru is your friend. In that case, he could be called a spiritual friend. If you don't think your guru is your friend, but instead he is a spiritual cop [that is not so good].

STUDENT: The tantric practice of visualization comes across as a kind of supertechnique as compared to hinayana and mahayana techniques.

TRUNGPA RINPOCHE: Sure. The vajrayana mentality knows how to work with your basic being. The vajrayana approach is supposedly the highest way there is of relating with your psychology. It is more developed than the hinayana and mahayana. It is the highest, most refined and powerful technique that mankind, or even nonmankind, could ever think of. That's precisely the point: it's superfantastic. That's why it is called the vajrayana, the diamond vehicle, as opposed to just the small or big vehicle. It is a vehicle carved out of diamond.

STUDENT: Is there any correlation between the five buddha families and the different yanas?

TRUNGPA RINPOCHE: I don't think so. All the yanas have a connection with all the five buddha families. The five buddha principles are the inhabitants, and the yanas are different countries—more advanced and less advanced countries.

STUDENT: I'm not sure how to relate to my basic nature in terms of the five buddha families. When I look at myself, I see not just one of them but parts of all of them. It's very confusing.

TRUNGPA RINPOCHE: The important point is to have some kind of trust in your basic nature. Your style is not regarded as a mistake or derived from some original sin of some kind. Your style is pure and obvious. When you doubt your style, you begin to develop another style, which is called an exit. You begin to manifest yourself in a different fashion, to try to shield your own style to make sure it is not discovered by other people.

I think as far as basic nature is concerned, there is no mistake at all. That is where vajra pride comes in. In the vajrayana approach, you are what you are. If you're passionate, that's beautiful. If you're aggressive, that's beautiful. If you're ignorant, that's beautiful. And all the materials and manifestations in you are regarded as in the vajra realm, rather than your being condemned as a failure. The whole thing is really highly workable. That is why it is called the diamond vehicle. Because what goes on in your life is not rejected or selected.

STUDENT: Is there one way we are, or are we all of those ways?

TRUNGPA RINPOCHE: Well, one way is the convention. Vajra pride is the one way. Take pride in yourself.

STUDENT: When you talk about not rejecting what goes on in your life, or when you talk about mahamudra as the world presenting messages or symbols—like when you're speeding, you get arrested—that just seems like common sense. It just seems like common sense that there are those kinds of messages. So it is not clear what the special quality is of working with those kinds of messages in the vajrayana.

TRUNGPA RINPOCHE: I don't see any difference, actually. It's just pure common sense. But the message that comes out of that should be a firsthand account rather than a secondhand one.

S: Well, how do the practices you've described, such as visualization of Mahavairochana, connect to the common sense of responding to messages in your life?

TR: The visualizations are also common sense. That is the whole point. You are not having a foreign culture imposed on you or awkward ideas presented to you. Even the visualizations themselves are common sense. Yes, that's true. Because the visualizations have something to do with you. That's why different aspects of the five buddha principles become your *yidams*.[4] *Yid* means "mind," and *dam* means "trust." Your mind can trust in certain particular aspects of the five buddha principles. You might be related with vajra Mahavairochana, ratna Mahavairochana, padma Mahavairochana, karma Mahavairochana, or buddha Mahavairochana. You can relate with certain particular principles and visualize them. It is like visualizing yourself. That's the whole point of the yidam—it means that you have a personal relationship with that principle. Those things are not given out haphazardly, like saying everybody should eat peanut butter and jelly because it's cheap and good for everybody.

STUDENT: In your lineage, are those practices, those visualizations, considered transmissions from the teachers to students, or can one read about them in books and practice from that?

TRUNGPA RINPOCHE: You can't get it from books. It might be written about in books, but books are just menus. You can't get a good meal just by reading the menu. You have to relate with the chef. We are the chefs. You can't get a good [spiritual] meal out of a pamphlet.

S: So when you speak here about those visualizations, are you giving a transmission to the group about how to do it?

TR: I'm presenting my point of view. There are already things happening in America relating to this material. A lot of visualizations and ideas have already been shared and publicized. So I'm just presenting what I have to say as guidelines. We are all working toward the same goal. At the same time, however, I'm giving a warning. I'm saying that the food could be poisonous if you don't relate with it properly.

Also what I'm doing here is presenting these ideas as appetizers, not to convert you, so that you become Tibetan Buddhists, but there is that possibility if you would like to get into this thing. It is a highly beautiful, fantastic trip. Better than any other trip you have ever gone through. This is a tripless trip, and a sensible and a good one as well.

Yes, I'm the chef.

STUDENT: How do the visualizations relate to craziness?

TRUNGPA RINPOCHE: They are related because the visualizations are crazy too. They are outrageous.

STUDENT: Is a visualization a visual experience or a heart experience?

TRUNGPA RINPOCHE: A heart experience. If you relate with visualizations as technicolor visual things, that's a problem. You might end up being Rudra. Or a superape, as we mentioned earlier. If you relate to the visualization as just a sense of inspiration that you have, that is when you are first getting a heart experience altogether.

STUDENT: Are the buddha families complementary? Particularly, if you are thinking of connecting with someone as a marriage partner or a lover, should the partner be the same type or a different type?

TRUNGPA RINPOCHE: It's like the four seasons. Summer does not get married to winter without going through autumn. The same thing applies here. Autumn would prefer to get married to winter, and winter would like to marry spring. And so forth. It's an organic situation.

STUDENT: How do the five aspects of buddha nature relate to ego?

TRUNGPA RINPOCHE: That's the whole point. Those buddha principles are ego's style as well as transcending ego. They are not just higher goals. They are something we can work with while we are here.

8

Anuttara Yoga

The next yana is the yoga yana, which our time does not permit us to go into in great detail. The view of the yoga yana is quite similar to that of the preceding yana, upa yoga yana. The sense of the practice is also fairly similar, but the relationship to the deity is more direct. There is more sense of union with the divine element—the meaning of *yoga* is "union."

At this point I would like primarily to discuss *anuttara yoga* [which emerges as the supreme level at this point]. It goes beyond the perspective on reality of the kriya yoga yana—purity—and that of the upa yoga yana, which is a sense of bringing action and experience together, as well as beyond the sense of union with the deity of the yoga yana. The Tibetan for *anuttara* is *la-me,* which literally means "none higher." *La* means "higher," and *me* means "not"; so there is nothing higher than this. Anuttara is the highest experience that one can ever relate with. There is a sense of personal involvement. The experience of tantra is extremely personal, rather than purely philosophical, spiritual, or religious. In general, there is really a definite sense of something personal. The reason that anuttara yoga is regarded as the highest of all is that the sense that everything is the mind's creation, a mental projection, is dropped. From the point of view of anuttara, everything is what is, rather than purely the consequence of certain causal characteristics based on purity or impurity. As far as anuttara is concerned, there is no notion of causal characteristics, or chain reactions, or ecological consequences. Things are based on *as-it-is*. The chain reactions have their own basic nature; even the results of the chain reactions are as they are, and that is what you relate to, so you don't have origins or results or fruition of things at all. Things are cut-and-dried, so to speak. Things are straightforward, definitely straightforward—direct and precise.

There is something that we haven't yet discussed with regard to the tantric tradition, which applies to all levels of it: kriya, upa, yoga, anuttara, and so forth. That is the transmitter of the tantric strength or energy to the student—the importance of the vidyadhara. The vidyadhara is the holder of crazy wisdom, which in Tibetan is *yeshe chölwa*. *Yeshe* means "wisdom," and *chölwa* is "gone wild"; so it is the wisdom gone wild, crazy wisdom. The holder of crazy wisdom, yeshe chölwa, scientific knowledge, is the guru, the spiritual master. The tantric approach to the guru also applies to the kriya yoga yana, the upa yoga yana, the yoga yana—whatever tantric yana we talk about. The notion of the teacher is quite different from that of the bodhisattva level. On the bodhisattva level, the teacher is regarded as a ferryman. The idea of a ferryman is that he has to save his own life as well as care for his fellow passengers. Therefore there is a mutual understanding, a sympathetic approach, a sense of fighting a common enemy. The *kalyanamitra*, or "spiritual friend" in Sanskrit, from the mahayana point of view is the friend who saves you, the driver of the vehicle, the charioteer, or the pilot of the ship. Such a pilot is also in danger if he doesn't operate the ship properly. His life is equally at risk as those of the passengers. That is the mahayana tradition. But in tantra, we have the notion of the warrior we discussed earlier on. The guru, the spiritual master, has tremendous power and also possesses a lot of understanding regarding the situation he is dealing with. From the tantric point of view, the spiritual friend is no longer a spiritual friend. From the tantric point of view, the guru is a dictator—in the benevolent sense—who minds every step of your life experience and who also demands faith and trust in the context of the bondage of the samaya vow.

The Tibetan word for *samaya* is *tamtsik,* which literally means "sacred word." *Tam* means "sacred," and *tsik* means "word." A samaya vow is a sacred word. It has the significance of the student and the guru having a mutual experience. The guru's action is within the realm of sacredness, and the student's involvement in the tradition of the teaching is also sacred. Therefore there is mutual sacredness.

The guru is regarded as a buddha in the flesh, a buddha in a human body. The guru is the herukas; the guru is the definite manifestation of divine principles of all kinds. That is why when you are accepted into the tantric tradition you take certain abhishekas or empowerments from the guru. This is an important commitment that you make to the tantric tradition. It is in some sense comparable to confirmation in the Christian tradition, or anointment [in the biblical tradition]. Or maybe it is similar to the Jewish tradition of bar mitzvah. From that day onward, you are accepted into the circle of the grownups on the tantric level.

Abhishekas are popularly referred to as initiations. This is the wrong translation. The idea of initiation into a certain tribal status is not necessarily applicable. Translating *abhisheka* that way is not an accurate use of language. Nevertheless it gives some general idea. You are initiated into this particular creed, particular dogma, by the father or chief of the tribe, who executes the ceremony. In this case, the guru's role is that of a warrior chief who puts you through all kinds of trials. You can't just be initiated pleasantly, delightfully, smoothly. You have to be made to face certain challenges in which you are made aware of the phenomenal world.

Do you remember a movie called *A Man Called Horse?* The hero of that movie had to go through a whole process of acceptance into the tribal system. He had to go through all kinds of training, excruciating trials and challenges, until finally he saw himself in a vision. He saw himself in a vision seeing a vision of himself, and so forth. [In a similar way, when you are introduced to the tantric tradition,] you begin to realize who you are and what you are. It is an interesting analogy. The spiritual friend turns into a tribal chief, who begins to mind your business much more heavy-handedly than you expected on the bodhisattva level. It's extremely heavy-handed.

This applies to the tantric tradition generally. What we have been discussing is not a unique quality of anuttara yoga. We are discussing the general tantric approach to life, particularly as concerns the teacher or transmitter. We are discussing the need for devotion to the guru in the tantric tradition.

In Hinduism, which is a theistic tradition, devotion to the guru is very conveniently developed as devotion to God, or Brahman. The guru is the only link between you and God. God is that mysterious thing out there. He or she, or whatever, is there already, and in order for you to find out whether God is a he or a she, the guru has to tell you; only he can tell you what God is.

A similar approach developed in Christianity. Jehovah could be communicated with only through Christ, so one should worship the latter. Worship the spoon and fork and plate, which is related with the food. The link between you and the food is the spoon. You have to hold it in a certain meditative or contemplative way. You have to hold it with a certain discipline, represented by your hand. The hand of devotional practice relates with faith to the spoon, which is Christ. Christ, the spoon, relates with the food, which is Jehovah.

In the Buddhist approach, the idea of an external being is completely ignored. It is regarded as an extremely crude, primitive idea. You do not need an interpreter to translate the language of god into the language of human beings. The function of the guru, from the Buddhist point of view, is to communicate the sense of the mysteriousness of the world, to communicate to you the sense of reality from the Buddhist point of view. This is the nontheistic or atheistic approach of tantra. Your spiritual friend, who in this case is a benevolent dictator who minds your business, relates to you. The consequences of deception, passion, or ignorance are great, so you have to keep yourself within the bounds of law and order. You have to try to tune yourself in to the law and order of the cosmic kingdom. But there is no question of the guru functioning as a divine messenger. The guru is the sensible teacher, sensible scientist. He almost has the quality of a sensible attorney, your lawyer, who tells you how to handle your life. But in this case, we do not pay the attorney money; we pay our guru-attorney with faith and trust.

That seems to be a natural situation if we are in trouble. We are highly involved with our troubles. We are actually absolutely fucked up and helpless, desperate, so we begin to relate with the guru as our attorney. If we were not all that fucked up, we might think the attorney was rejectable, not indispensable; we might have a lighthearted relationship with our attorney. But spiritually, we are definitely completely fucked up in any case, in a complete mess, because we do not know who we are or what we are, let alone what we might be. We can't develop any argument, because we are uncertain who is arguing, who is putting our case; so we are absolutely fucked up. We do need our attorney very badly, extremely badly.

In the tantric tradition, the sense of guru plays an extremely important part. The reason why the guru plays an important part is that you are desperate. And when you commit yourself into a more involved situation like tantric discipline, the guru's word is regarded as absolute supertruth, not just ordinary old truth, but vajra truth, truth with power behind it.[1] If you reject such a truth, you can get hurt, you can be destroyed. So you commit yourself to the guru in a threefold way. The form of the guru is regarded as a self-existing manifestation of the truth in the search for the basic sanity of vajrayana. The speech of the guru is regarded as a mantra, a proclamation; anything from him on the sound or intellectual level is absolutely accurate. If you doubt that, you can get hurt, destroyed, your intuition can get cut down. And the mind of the guru is cosmic mind. If you doubt his mind, again you can get hurt, because you could end up suffering from insanity, a fundamental freak-out of ego.

The tantric tradition places tremendous importance on the transmitter, the guru. He plays an extremely important part in all this. The form, speech, and mind of the guru have to be respected and surrendered to. You have to be willing to relate with that absolutely, 100 percent. You are entering the fundamentally sane situation of a benevolent dictator. Once we tread on the path of tantric practice, we switch from the bodhisattva's world of kindness and gentleness and democracy to the realm of the benevolent dictator. The guru plays an extremely important part in this whole thing. If you disobey the guru's message on the level of form, speech, or mind, you are struck, you go straight to vajra hell.

Getting involved with the vajrayana without preparation seems to have extremely dangerous and powerful consequences. That is why I personally feel that introducing tantric practice to this country prematurely could be destructive for individuals and their development rather than a help. At this point, the practice of students studying with me is at the level of basic Buddhism: hinayana with an element of mahayana. We haven't gotten into the kill-or-cure level of tantra yet. Hopefully we will be able to get into that in the very near future.

I think there are something like 750 vows that have developed in the tantric discipline of samaya, *samaya shila,* and all of these are based on the guru.[2] If you mistreat the guru, if you have doubt about the guru, if you have a vengeful attitude toward the guru, you might be struck. Before you enter into samaya shila, the guru gives you the water of the samaya oath, and you drink it. Once you have drunk it, this water will either become a saving grace, helping toward the development of basic sanity, or it will turn into an absolute atomic bomb. You could be killed, destroyed in the direst manner one could ever imagine, in vajra hell.

Of course the idea of introducing tantra into this country is very exciting, but the consequences of the problems involved in tantra are very scary. People should be told the dangers of tantra rather than the advantages—that you could learn to walk in the air or fly, or develop inner heat, a central heating system—all those little things you think about. It's like thinking about what you will do when you become a millionaire. You can buy a Mercedes or a Jaguar and have all kinds of penthouses to live in. But that's not the point. Rather than thinking about how to become a millionaire, we should think about the dangers of becoming a millionaire. That is the problem we are facing.

At all levels of tantra, you need a transmitter to transmit this spiritual power. This power can be turned into something good or bad, powerful or destructive. An analogy that developed in Tibet is that entering tantric discipline is like putting a poisonous snake in a bamboo pipe. The snake might go either up or down. Once one has begun to relate with tantra, there is no compromise, no happy medium; there's no Madhyamaka, no middle way. There's no happy system of compromise anymore at all. Once you get into tantric discipline, you either go up or you go down. Either you become buddha or you become Rudra, a cosmic monster.

The basic point of anuttara yoga is trying to relate with the abhisheka principles that are found on all tantric levels. In this way, finally we begin to relate with the mahamudra principle we discussed earlier. We have a sense that it can be realized and worked with. There is no doubt about anything at all. The mahamudra principle can be seen and felt, and in consequence there's no doubt with regard to any of the tantric symbolism, the iconography of herukas and dakinis. Those symbols become very straight and direct—a real manifestation of your buddha nature can come through you. You are able to face it, to relate with it in the form of a heruka, a yidam. If your nature is vajra, you can relate with vajra nature; if you're padma, you can relate with padma nature. You have no doubt about the fact that that particular principle involved in life situations is workable, very powerful. You can relate with it and transcend [any doubts].

At this point the divine quality is no longer a foreign element. Your own existence also becomes a divine element. You begin to experience the highest point of vajra pride and the highest point of the mahamudra principle. All the mudras, or signs, that are seen in life situations also become something you can relate with, work with. Things become more vivid and more precise and extraordinarily powerful. At last we become able to solve the mystery of the cosmic games. Games are no longer games and jokes are no longer jokes. I think one of the basic points of anuttara yoga is that the world is seen as workable, no longer a mystery. Mysticism has profundities, as we know; but at the anuttara yoga level, those are no longer a mystery. They are something you can relate with and work with. The wetness of water is a direct message. The hotness of fire is a direct message. There is no longer any mystery involved.

Through understanding the whole thing, we begin to trust our world, to realize that there is no such thing as a cosmic conspiracy. The world is a rational world, a kind world, there's no joke involved. It is a workable situation. So we could say that the quality of the anuttara yoga level is the realization that the world is a safe world, a kind world, that the world is not trying to make a mockery of you—which is what we generally think until we reach this point.

Generally we think there is some trickery involved, that we should try to be smarter than what's happening. We should at least try to make sure that we are not conned by the situations of our life. We should be much smarter, more cunning. But at this point we realize that [counter-] conmanship is unnecessary, which is the highest discovery ever made by mankind. All sentient beings can realize that. If you realize that you don't have to con anybody, that is the ultimate anuttara yoga indeed. We don't have to con anybody, including ourselves.

STUDENT: You say at a certain point the world is realized to be a benevolent, kind world. My immediate reaction to that is, how could that be? The forces of nature seem to be indifferent. If we have an earthquake right now, is that regarded as the manifestation of a kind and benevolent world?

TRUNGPA RINPOCHE: Mm-hmmm.

S: That seems pretty farfetched.

TR: At this point, your mind has not been trained to realize anuttara yoga, that's why.

S: I still don't see it. If there's an earthquake, who is the recipient of that kindness?

TR: Nobody.

S: Then who is it that calls it kind?

TR: You do.

S: As I'm swallowed up by a crack in the earth?

TR: That's your trip. You produce the teaching. You create Buddhism yourself. There's no Buddhism as such; you produce it by yourself. You want to relate with Buddhism rather than the samsaric world. You produce nirvana, because you experience samsara; it's your trip. The tantric tradition speaks in a much more powerful way than the hinayana or the mahayana when it says that it's your trip. The earthquake is a good message, saying that this is your world, which you produced, and it is highly energetic and powerful.

STUDENT: You were talking about the relationship between teacher and student, which you said was based on trust. In your poetry, if I have understood it properly, you say emphatically, do not trust, do not trust. Is that trust that's necessary for the relationship between student and teacher the same thing as "do not trust"?

TRUNGPA RINPOCHE: I think so; not trusting is the saving grace. When you do not trust, you're distrustful; then there is some continuity. It is precisely in that sense that the mahayanist talks about the emptiness of everything. Emptiness is the truth in reality; it is wisdom. If you trust in the emptiness, nonexistence, if you are distrustful in that way, that is continual trust. There's some kind of faith involved at the same time.

STUDENT: You used the word *divine* a few times in this talk. At what point in the progression from hinayana to mahayana to vajrayana does that word start to become relevant?

TRUNGPA RINPOCHE: The divine or divinity or benevolence can only be relevant if there is no perceiver of them. In other words, god can be a legitimate experience if there is no watcher of the god. The god can only be perceived if there is no worshiper of the god. In other words, Jehovah does exist as a workable experience if there are no Christians, no Jews, no Christ.

STUDENT: It seems that we are practicing the hinayana and mahayana, but you are starting to teach us tantra in the middle of that.

TRUNGPA RINPOCHE: A very important point is that we could relate with the vajrayana and mahayana levels in relation to how to handle our life situation. As far as practice itself is concerned, [at this point] we should relate purely with the hinayana with maybe just a little pinch of mahayana. Our beliefs have to be destroyed through the rationale of hinayana Buddhism. But our relationship to our life activity could involve taking a chance. That has to be raised from the simpleminded level of hinayana to the mahayana and vajrayana levels if possible.

STUDENT: Could you say something about what a karmic debt is?

TRUNGPA RINPOCHE: That seems to be very simple. If we decide to re-create either good or bad activities, we are going to get involved with the results of that. Then, by getting involved with those results, we sow a further seed as well. It is like seeing a friend once; having lunch with your friend sows seeds for having another lunch with your friend. And so you go on and on *and* on and on.

STUDENT: I'm a little mixed up about something. If you don't get to the tantric level before having gone through the hinayana and the mahayana, after you've gone through the hinayana and mahayana, why should you still be so fucked up that you need the guru-dictator?

TRUNGPA RINPOCHE: You do need that; that's precisely the point. You probably have accomplished and achieved a lot, but still you could be carrying the neurosis of the hinayana and the mahayana. You need someone to destroy those. They are very powerful, highly spiritually materialistic, extremely powerful— and you need to be cut down. You create wisdom by being involved with the hinayana and you create the hang-ups that go along with it. Then when you get involved in the mahayana, you create further wisdom, greater wisdom, paramita wisdom, but you also create paramita hang-ups as well. Those things have to be cut down by the dictator, the guru, and that principle is much higher and more powerful still. There's no end. There's no end, my dear friend.

STUDENT: With this feeling of commitment you were transmitting with regard to tantra, I got a feeling of desperation at the same time. That made me wonder: is there also more of a feeling of egolessness at the tantric level, when it comes time to make that commitment? Does the student have less watcher at that point?

TRUNGPA RINPOCHE: I think so. But at the same time, there will also be the problem of the hang-ups that this lady [the previous questioner] and I were just discussing. That happens as well. That goes on right up until maha ati yoga, which comes at the end of the seminar. You should hear that as well.

STUDENT: You were saying that tantric practices have been prematurely introduced into this country and that they lead to a loss of individuality, or something like that, if they are introduced too early. Could you elaborate?

TRUNGPA RINPOCHE: I think that tantra has been introduced too early in this country, definitely. Particularly, some of the Hinduism. Hinduism is tantra. There is no hinayana aspect to Hinduism as it has been presented in this country. In Hinduism as it exists in India, before you become a *sannyasin*, or renunciate, before you become a tantric practitioner involved with the religious tradition, you raise your children, you work on your farm, and you relate with your country. That is the equivalent of hinayana in Hinduism. That hasn't been introduced in this country. Only the glamorous part of Hinduism, the cream of it, which infants can't handle, has been introduced here. Students of Hinduism have not really been mature enough. Hinduism is a nationalistic religion. In order to become a Hindu, you have to become a good citizen of India, raise your children, cook good food, be a good father or mother—all those things. This is similar to what developed in Judaism. It seems that the problem we're facing is that without that basic grounding, highlights have been introduced that are extraordinarily electric and powerful. As a result, people have suffered a lot, because they are not even on the level of relating with their families, their parents. Many people have decided to regard their parents as enemies. There's no solid social structure. They decide they dislike their mother's cooking. They'd rather go to a restaurant than taste their mother's cooking. There's no sacredness in their relationship to their family. Maybe that's why there are so many restaurants around here.

That seems to be a problem, actually, sociologically or spiritually. The Hinduism that has been introduced in this country is highly powerful, extremely mystical. It is at the level of tantra. But there has been no hinayana introduced that relates with how to behave.

STUDENT: I feel very much what you say about the danger of leaping over something that is supposed to be done first. I just wonder whether it has to do with the speed-up of time that is going on. I feel right now that everything is happening with incredible speed. Everybody walks fast. And I wonder how that can be brought into connection with a tradition that has gone through centuries. It is dangerous to get into tantra without going through hinayana and mahayana, but everybody, particularly in America, wants instant nirvana.

TRUNGPA RINPOCHE: I think that is because America has actually achieved a materialistic vajrayana, and Americans expect to get a spiritual equivalent. Because they're so spoiled. There's automation, and everything is materialistically highly developed. They have gone through the hinayana level of manual farming and so on, and the mahayana level of creating a republican, democratic society as the American world. They take pride in taking the pledge [of allegiance], worshiping the flag, and so forth, on a mahayana level of benevolence. Then beyond that, they have also achieved the vajrayana level of automation, and there are all kinds of power trips and all kinds of war materiel—missiles, bombs, airplanes—everything has been achieved on a vajrayana level. And now that they're so spoiled on that level, they are asking for the spiritual equivalent of that. They don't want to go back to the hinayana level. They have everything happening to their lives, so they are asking direct: "We have everything we want materially, therefore we want everything we want spiritually too." That is tantric materialism, spiritual tantric materialism. That seems to be the problem, and if there are any wise tantric teachers around, Americans won't get it.

STUDENT: Would you say that most drug trips are tantric spiritual materialism?

TRUNGPA RINPOCHE: No. The drug trips, LSD and so forth, are not as tantric as they think they are. It is purely on the level of mahayana materialism. The idea is that drugs are good for society, because they provide good vibrations, goodness and love, and realization leading to goodness. So the drug culture could be described as mahayana rather than tantric.

STUDENT: Traditionally, surrender to the spiritual friend was enabled by the all-encompassing love the student had for the spiritual friend. That enabled the student to have faith and trust in him. Is there any room for that?

TRUNGPA RINPOCHE: I think there's room for everything—your emotions and your trust and everything. That is what ideal devotion is: your emotions and your trust and everything else is involved. It's a big deal, 100 percent. That's why the samaya vow with the guru is the most important discipline in tantra. Without respecting your guru, you can't get tantric messages.

There's the story of Marpa visiting Naropa. Naropa had magically created a vision of the mandala of Hevajra, with the colors and everything, above the altar.[3] Then Naropa asked Marpa, "Would you like to prostrate to the mandala, or would you like to prostrate to the guru?" Marpa thought that the guru's magical creation was a fantastic discovery. He thought he would rather prostrate to the divine existence he could see, so he decided to prostrate to the magic show. He did that, and Naropa said, "You're out! You didn't place your trust in me, the creator of the whole show. You didn't prostrate to me, you prostrated to my manifestation. You still have to work harder."

So it's a question of whether to worship the magical achievement or the magician himself. The guru is, in fact, from the tantric point of view, the magician. Even in relation to our rational twentieth-century minds, the guru has all kinds of magic. Not that the guru produces elephants out of the air or turns the world upside down, but the guru has all kinds of ordinary magic. It is seemingly ordinary, but it is also irritating, unpleasant, surprising, entertaining, and so forth.

STUDENT: What is the difference between the guru and the Christian godhead?

TRUNGPA RINPOCHE: In the Christian approach, God is unreachable. The guru is immediate. For one thing, he is a human being like yourself. He has to eat food and wear clothes like you do, so it's a direct relationship. And the fact that the guru has basic human survival needs makes the situation more threatening. Do you see what I mean? It is more threatening because you can't dismiss the guru as being outside of our thing, someone who can survive without our human trips. The guru does thrive on human trips. If we need food, the guru also needs food. If we need a love affair, the guru also needs a love affair. A guru is an ordinary human being, but still powerful. We begin to feel personally undermined, because the guru minds our trips too closely and too hard. That is why the guru is powerful: he asks you what food you eat and what clothes you wear. He minds your business on those levels as well as with regard to your relationships, your practice, your body, your job, your house. The guru involves himself with those things more and more. Whereas if he were God, he would just be hanging out somewhere. God doesn't make any personal comments, except in terms of your conscience—which is your fantasy anyway.

STUDENT: Rinpoche, at one point when you were describing mahayana, you said that there's a role for doubt in mahayana. You said that there's a confluence of the river of the teaching and the river of doubt, and that by contrast, tantra was like a single thread. Does that mean that there's no role or function for doubt once you enter tantra? Is it completely eliminated?

TRUNGPA RINPOCHE: That's precisely where the dictatorship comes in. You are not allowed to have any doubt. If you have doubts, they'll be cut. Doubt is not regarded as respectable in tantric society.

9

Mahamudra and Maha Ati

It seems necessary at this point to clarify the classification of the tantric yanas. There is a gradual psychological evolution or development through the first three levels of kriya, upa, and yoga. Then there is a fourth stage of tantra in relation to that group known as anuttara yoga. This is the classification of the tantric yanas according to the New Translation school that existed in Tibet.

The New Translation school is particularly associated with the mahamudra teaching. The reason it is called the New Translation school is to distinguish it from the Old Translation school, the tradition associated with the maha ati teachings of tantra, which were introduced into Tibet earlier on, at the time of Padmasambhava. The maha ati teachings are connected with the mahayoga, anuyoga, and atiyoga yanas, which we will be discussing.[1]

The New Translation school started with Marpa and other great translators who reintroduced tantra into Tibet later on. This later tantric school developed the teachings of Naropa and Virupa, two Indian siddhas. The teachings of Naropa particularly influenced the Gelug and Kagyü tantric traditions in Tibet, and the teachings of Virupa particularly influenced the tantric tradition of the Sakya order of Tibet.[2]

As I said, the mahamudra teaching is connected with the new tantric tradition, the New Translation school. The predominant meditation practice in the kriya, upa, yoga, and anuttara yoga yanas is mahamudra. We discussed mahamudra earlier, but I think maybe we have to go over it more.

First we have to develop the clear perception that comes from removing the dualistic barrier in accordance with the notion of shunyata. This is the experience or insight of the bodhisattva. Having removed the obstacles or fog of that barrier, one begins to have a clear perception of the phenomenal world as it is. That is the mahamudra experience. It's not that mahayana only cuts through the dualistic barrier—it also re-creates our sense of richness; we have a sense of appreciating the world again, once more, without preconceptions, without any barrier.

In a sense the shunyata experience could be described as a totally negative experience, that of cutting down, cutting through. It is still involved with a sense of struggle. In some sense you could say that shunyata needs a reference point. The reference point of the barrier between self and other creates the reference point of nonbarrier. The mahamudra principle does not even need the barrier to express itself or anything else at all to go against. It is just a pure, straightforward expression of the world of sight and smell and touchable objects as a self-existing mandala experience. There is no inhibition at all. Things are seen precisely, beautifully, without any fear of launching into them.

Within that experience of mahamudra is clear perception—we could use that expression: "clear perception." In this case, clear perception is the experience of the five wisdoms of the five buddha families. There is clear perception of the mirrorlike wisdom of the vajra family, seeing things precisely and sharp-edged. They appear methodical; everything's in order. There is also the wisdom of discriminating awareness of the padma family: you begin to relate with a sense of perspective and relationship—in other words, there is a sense of sorting out. The vajra aspect, the mirrorlike wisdom, is just precision, a vision; the discriminating awareness wisdom of padma is more discriminatory, more of a sorting-out process. Then the wisdom of equanimity of ratna provides a general background in relation to which everything is workable, everything is dealt with, nothing is missing. Then the wisdom of the fulfillment of all actions of the karma family is the driving force behind that makes it possible for wisdom to be put into practice. And then there is the wisdom of dharmadhatu, of all-encompassing space, of the buddha family in which nothing is rejected. Absolutely everything is included in the experience, both samsara and nirvana, or anything that one can imagine at all.

The five wisdoms are somewhat connected with a sense of wildness, in the style of the crazy yogi. Fundamentally, in anuttara yoga's approach to life, there is no need for careful examination. Within those wisdoms, things are already sorted out. That is precisely what we mean by *mandala:* things are already sorted out. They are in perspective already; they don't have to be sorted out. Things are seen as ordinary. Chaos is orderly chaos. Things might appear chaotic, but there is a pattern, there is an order. So, from that point of view, there is no reason for the crazy yogi to be careful—things are already worked out.

This is not just purely blind faith, a matter of just jumping in. Rather it is a matter of seeing things in the right perspective so that you have no reason to be doubtful. Moreover, you have a relationship with a master or teacher, a person who pushes you if you are in doubt. So personal conviction in the teaching, in the wisdoms, and the close guidance of the teacher gives birth to the crazy yogi.

Crazy in this case means having no need to look twice. One flash of experience is enough, and it is a real flash of experience, of seeing the world in the light of wisdom, in the light of mahamudra. Everything happens in your life situation; even if you forget to acknowledge it, life comes to you and acknowledges you. So it's a perpetual development: practice goes on even in the absent-minded state. The teaching goes on; the learning process goes on.

We could say that that is the highest experience that anuttara can achieve. If you are studying a particular sadhana with a particular heruka, then in your life situation just as in the rest of your practice, the forms that you perceive are the images of the heruka, the sounds you hear are the voice of the heruka, and anything that occurs in the realm of the mind is the wisdom of the heruka.

Of course this does not necessarily mean that you start seeing pictures or that you re-create heaven. You see the traffic lights as traffic lights, and you see dollar bills as dollar bills. But they all have some vajrayana quality behind them, a vajra quality. A vajra quality in this case is the sense that things are very rich; even the function of just a grain of sand is a rich one. A broken bottle on the street, or some dog shit—whatever—is the vajra nature; the vajra quality is in them. I'd prefer not to use the word *divine* here, because when we use the word *divine* there is a sense of softness and a sense of a hierarchical setup. But when we use the word *vajra,* it does not have a hierarchical connotation. There's no feeling of saving grace or a higher or greater being; but it is a sharp and precise and highly profound experience. In that way, on the tantric level of practice, whatever happens in our life situation, the whole thing becomes the expression of the heruka or of mahamudra experience.

But still that is not the ultimate experience. There is more to go. We might wonder: if you have cut the dualistic barrier and you perceive the world as it is in the light of wisdom, and if, so to speak, you can dance with the gods and goddesses and converse with them in the most practical, simple way, what more could you want? It sounds great. But still there is something that doesn't click. There is still the sense of an experience. There's still a sense of a commuter, a back-and-forth journey, as all-pervasive as it might be, as serene and clear and tranquil as it may be, still it's experience. Still it's mudra, still it's message, still this is the truth, still this is the ultimate. All of those contain a reference point.

Still this is regarded as the perfect one, and that seems to be the problem. We have three more yanas to go, and those three yanas, which are in the maha ati category, cut through those reference points.

Ati is called the end. It is called *dzokpa chenpo* in Tibetan, which means the great ending. It is a gigantic full stop, rather than a beginning. The three yanas connected with the maha ati experience have to do with transcending reference point altogether. This means abandoning the idea of wisdom as opposed to confusion or being a fool. We cannot just cut on the level of language; we can't just start from the outside. Something has to happen right within.

As far as perceiving the herukas or relating with them is concerned, they have to be more terrifying or more peaceful. Even the reference point of logic cannot describe their extreme existence or the extreme experience of them. They are so extreme that even the word *extreme* does not apply anymore. It is a fathomless experience.

The first yana on the ati level is the mahayoga yana. This is something beyond anuttara. When this yoga speaks of the ultimate power, it is in destroying the notion of power. When it speaks of the ultimate enlightenment, it is in beginning to destroy enlightenment, not just the enlightenment concept but enlightenment itself. What we have been doing so far is finding holes in some aspect of the teaching, then laying a heavy trip on that as being conceptual. We have been finding our scapegoat that way. So we have gotten rid of the concept, but we haven't gotten rid of the conceptualizer. Even on the level of subtlety we have reached by this yana, we still hang on to it. Even somebody who has achieved the highest form of mahamudra still hangs on to that logic, that style of dealing with oneself. So at this point we are destroying the destroyer and destroying the creator; or we could express it positively and talk about creating the creator and destroying the destroyer. That doesn't matter. That's not the point. There are no positive or negative things involved, no negation and no affirmation.

That seems to bring us to a glimpse of crazy wisdom as opposed to just the crazy yogi. There seems to be a difference between the two. The yogi is a practitioner and has the reference point of the spiritual journey. The yogi is still moving toward the goal, still walking on the path as a practitioner. He is still wise, but his wisdom is different from crazy wisdom. As we have already said, crazy wisdom in Tibetan is *yeshe chölwa,* wisdom run wild. That's the ultimate form of craziness, which is the highest form of sanity, needless to say. That is because it does not believe in any extremes at all, or rather doesn't dwell on them—because belief is very primitive, and after belief is destroyed, you dwell on that achievement.

The mahayoga yana is the introduction to the maha ati principle, the starting point for crazy wisdom. The yana after that, *anuyoga,* is basically the experience that sifts out the hang-ups of all the previous yanas and provides the potential for the final yana, which is ati. In that sense anuyoga could be regarded as the tantric version of a sieve. It completely and thoroughly sifts out dualistic notions, beliefs in even the highest spiritual subtleties.

To reach that point, however, we have to relate with the energy level of the world more completely, the energy of appreciating sight, smell, feeling, and so forth on the level of the mahayoga yana. The mahayoga yana is one of the best ways of creating a complete mandala and relating completely with the various heruka principles. In the mahayoga yana, there are what is known as the eight logos. *Logos* is the closest translation we can find for the Tibetan word *ka,* which also means "command" or "language." The eight logos can be laid out diagrammatically in a mandala. This involves a traditional way of relating with the directions, which is very similar to that found in the American Indian tradition. In this case, we start with the east and go clockwise.

Number one, then, in mahayoga yana's expression of the heruka principle, is associated with the east. The symbol of this heruka is a skull cup filled with oil with nine wicks in it. This acknowledges the mirrorlike wisdom of the vajra family, which is also connected with the east. In this case the purity and cleanness of vajra is not manifested as a peaceful deity—by no means. He is a wrathful one. This heruka's scepter is a round dagger, like a big pin with a spearhead. An ordinary dagger is flat and has one edge, but this is like a big pin that pierces any conceptual beliefs. The Tibetan name for that heruka is Yangdak. *Yang* means "once more" or "again." *Dak* means pure. The meaning of the two together is "complete purity." Once more, having already been through the hang-ups of the previous yanas, you have now reached the first exit toward the real meaning of freedom, toward the open air, direct toward outer space.

The next development is that of the south, number two. Here we have death, Yamantaka. This principle is associated with the owl, which has yellow eyes that see at night and has an acquaintance with darkness and death. This is quite different from the Westerner's idea of the owl as the bird of wisdom. Here the owl is associated with death because darkness is the owl's client. And death in this case is connected with the ratna family and considered an enrichment.

So the east is connected with vajra and one lamp with nine wicks, which is superluminous, like one torch with a hundred bulbs, each of a hundred watts. And then there is ratna as death, which is quite interesting. Usually we don't at all regard death as an enrichment. We regard death as a loss, a complete and tremendous loss. But here death is regarded as an enrichment—in the sense that the final cessation of existence could be regarded as the ultimate creativity. And the ultimate creativity or collecting process is also deathly at the same time. So there are those two polarities here. But by no means is relating with death, Yamantaka, regarded as something safe or something that will save you. Instead there is the interplay of those two polarities.

Then in the west, number three, there is the padma-family heruka, Hayagriva, who is related with passion. This is not passion in the sense of magnetizing alone, but also in the sense of proclaiming your passion. Hayagriva is associated with the horse, so Hayagriva's principle is referred to as the horse's neigh, the voice of the horse. The three neighs of that horse destroy the body, speech, and mind of Rudra. The symbol is a red lotus with flames as petals, a burning lotus, a burning heart, the proclamation of passion. But at the same time, this is a wrathful figure.

In the north, number four, is Vajrakilaya. *Kilaya* means "dagger." The kilaya is different from the dagger of the east, Yangdak's round dagger. The kilaya has one point but three edges. It is like a three-sided pyramid with sharpened corners. This represents the karma buddha family. It has the sense of penetration. The traditional idea of the karma family is purely functionality, the fulfillment of ends, achieving things, but in this case the karma principle has to do purely with penetration. This should not be confused with the intellectual penetration of the vajra family. The karma family of Vajrakilaya has to do with precision. Whereas vajra is intellectual, still surveying the area, karma is penetrating and accepts no nonsense.

Then you have the fifth one, which is associated with Chemchok in the center. This principle is connected with *amrita*, the anti-death potion. The symbol is a skull cup with liquor in it. Amrita, the best liquor, can only be brewed by the crazy-wisdom people. There is a sense of the transmutation of poison into medicine.

In the traditional sadhana practice connected with this principle, an accomplished guru and the sangha associated with him get together and brew a vajra liquor of eight main herbs and a thousand secondary ingredients. They ferment this mixture, which is called dharma medicine, in the presence of the shrine, and it is raised into liquor. Every process is a conscious one. When a person takes this alcoholic potion, the result is that hanging on to any of the yanas is freed.

I feel safe talking to this particular group about this, since they have some understanding of the hinayana, mahayana, and vajrayana principles. I think everybody here understands that they have to go through the whole training before they begin to "drop" amrita. So the transmutation of poison into medicine is connected with number five.

The next one, number six, is called "mother's curse," Mamo Bötong in Tibetan. Mother's curse in this case means that the phenomenal world begins to come into a closer relationship with you and your practice. You are in tune with the phenomenal world, and if you miss one second of relationship with the phenomenal world, you are cursed, bewitched. The symbol of the mother's curse is a bag full of liquid poison, with a snake as the rope fastening. This approach is so dangerous, extremely dangerous, and powerful at the same time. You can't miss an inch, a fraction of an inch, a fraction of a minute. If you are not in contact with anything, you can be destroyed instantaneously. Before you can think of being destroyed, it has already happened, and you go straight to vajra hell. The tantric approach, particularly the maha ati approach, is highly dictatorial. And it knows no limits. You are constantly under challenge.

The word *mother* is used here in the sense of the cosmic feminine principle, which is both seducer and destroyer. This is not on the messenger level, not just a warning. In actual solid situations, there is a difference between relating with the boss and relating with a messenger. Encountering the mother's curse is relating with the boss. If the boss dislikes you, dislikes your unskillful actions, he could really hurt you. There could be famine, war, madness, and all the rest of the worst consequences one could ever think of. But the mother's curse does not go too far. It is still at the facade level.

The next one, number seven, is Jikten Chötö in Tibetan. *Jikten* means "world," *chö* means "offer," and *tö* means "praise." We haven't practiced grounding ourselves in the world enough, so we have to praise our world, and also we have to offer our services to the world. This is a very interesting point, which seems to call for nationalism. A sense of nationalism is important. You don't regard your country as something to be abandoned or to be gotten rid of, as though you could step out of your country and enjoy another domain, another realm. So this seventh principle involves developing some basic nationalism. The place where you grew up, the place where you were raised and educated and where you are living, deserves some respect. Also, if you do not respect your country and take pride in your country, you might be struck, destroyed.

That is a very precise message, but we have little understanding of how to relate with our world, our nation. Americans have a problem relating with America. And national pride does not necessarily only mean worshiping the flag or the grand old presidents of the past, some of whom died peacefully and some of whom killed for the sake of the nation. That kind of nationalism is spiritual materialism. The kind of nationalism we are talking about is spiritual nationalism. Your country, where your belongings are and your life situation takes place, has spirituality, buddha nature in everything. This refers to the experience you have of your country, such as of the landscape—the beauty of America. Taking America as the basic image, let's suppose you went from California to Colorado to New York, and let's say you were walking instead of driving. You would begin to appreciate the beauty of your country enormously. It's almost fantastic: who thought up these ideas, such as that such a beautiful rock could be there, that beautiful plants could be there, that beautiful cactus could grow, and there could be such beautiful rolling hills and such beautiful maple leaves—all these things that your country churns out and nobody else's? We are talking about the very physical existence of the American land, the United States of America, or North America as a whole, including Canada. It could also be South America. But this land that you're living in is an extraordinarily beautiful one. It has glamorous cities, beautiful landscapes, and everything is unique. It is a complete world, which brings pride on the individual level as well as having subtleties and spiritual implications.

Your country is a really great country. There's very little need to take a trip to Tibet or visit Darjeeling to view the Himalayas. This is a tantric interpretation, a kind of vajra nationalism, which seems to be necessary at this point.

Then we have the last one, number eight, which is the principle of the ultimate spell, Möpa Trak-ngak in Tibetan. *Möpa* means "vicious," *trak* means "wrathful," and *ngak* means "mantra." This has the sense of "ultimate spell of wrathful action," which means that you are not afraid of striking anywhere, not afraid of challenging anything. If you have to sue somebody, you are willing to do it. You are not afraid of that. We have experienced the significance of that on the practical level. If you don't sue or take legal action against another party or an authority, you might end up economically as a zombie. So you have to take action.

This principle is a vajra curse or, better, a vajra incantation. We are not afraid to say that thus-and-such a person should be destroyed and thus-and-such a person should be developed. Which in fact is quite outrageous.

A lot of things that we encounter in these principles I feel the audience is trustworthy enough not to make into something else. This audience consists of good citizens rather than famous people, celebrities who might engage in wishful thinking about overpowering the nation. However, if someone did decide to make themselves important and try to rule the world or the nation, it's too late for them to do that. They could get struck.

Then we have anuyoga yana, which is connected with bringing the head and heart together on a practical level. You may have read in *The Tibetan Book of the Dead* that the peaceful deities are stationed in the heart chakra and the wrathful deities are stationed in the brain chakra. On the anuyoga yana level, a real relationship to the wrathful deities takes place, and they come alive. In the yanas associated with mahamudra, there is not enough emphasis on their wrathful aspect. Instead of being described as wrathful, they are described as threatening. The deities are described as threatening, passionate, and meditative in the mahamudra yanas. There are passionate ones with consorts or by themselves; the meditative ones are connected with ignorance; and the wrathful ones are described as threatening rather than wrathful. Threatening implies a certain objectivity—you can be threatening without losing your temper. Whereas in the case of the anuyoga yana, you have to lose your temper. You have to be 100 percent, if not 200 percent, into the wisdom. It is real anger rather than trying to play games skillfully.

Another aspect of the wrathful deities is that they have adopted the raiment of the Rudra of ego. They subjugate the Rudra of ego and use his clothing. This means not abandoning the samsaric world as something bad, but rather wearing it as an ornament.

The wrathful principle is connected with the brain, intellect. The peaceful deities are connected with the heart, emotion. The intellect in this case is not necessarily the analytical, rational mind. The intellect here is something aggressive in the vajra sense, something extremely powerful. This is the reason for the timing in *The Tibetan Book of the Dead:* first you see peaceful deities, and if they are not able to help you, then those peaceful deities turn into angry ones; they lose their temper and strike you again. In relation to the wrathful deities, the ati tantric tradition speaks of immense anger, without hatred of course, the most immense anger that enlightened mind could ever produce, as the most intense form of compassion. There is so much kindness and compassion in it that it turns red.

That is the expression of crazy wisdom. At this point there is no problem of maintaining balance. Extremes are used as the reference point of balance rather than any kind of compromises.

The leading mandala in the anuyoga yana is the one called the mandala of the hundred deities. It has forty-two peaceful divinities and fifty-eight wrathful deities related to the Vajrasattva principle, the principle of vajra nature. They all are manifestations of vajra nature—vajra passion and vajra anger.

It seems that we could discuss the iconographical symbolism connected with the growth in experience derived from the various yanas in great detail, but we don't have enough time. Also I feel responsible not to confuse you too much by introducing a lot of stuff—names and ideas. That might cause you to fail to see the general pattern, and you might become fascinated by the details.

So that brings us to the final yana, maha ati. The spiritual discipline of maha ati falls into four categories. The first one is the revelation of dharmata, which means reality. Here everything is seen as real and direct. The next one is called *nyam kongphel* in Tibetan. *Nyam* means "temporary experience," *kongphel* means to acknowledge your temporary experiences but not hang on to them. The next one is called *rikpa tsephep*. *Rikpa* means "intelligence," "intuition"; *tse* means "measure," and *phep* means "in accordance with that." You have reached a point of real perspective in your practice. The last one is "wearing out dharmata." Dharmata is the isness of all the dharmas constituted by both samsara and nirvana. So there is a wearing out of the whole thing; [you no longer prefer nirvana to samsara]. You are even giving up enlightenment.

One of the basic projects, if you can call it a project, on the maha ati level, and the point of all the practices that go on there, is to destroy the notion and the experience of enlightenment. So there's no goal, no search at all. That is what is called wearing out dharmata. And at that point there is a sense of being unleashed infinitely. There is a sense of craziness, the ultimate craziness, which does not believe in even trying to accomplish anything at all.

Usually when we feel crazy in the conventional, simpleminded way, it is because we have some political, spiritual, or domestic idea that we would like to communicate to the rest of the world. Therefore we feel crazy, dogmatic. In this case, there's a sense of being crazy and completely on the loose, but there's no game, no goal. That kind of crazy person doesn't have to say anything at all, or he could say a lot about the whole thing.

I feel that we cannot go too far with maha ati at this point. This is as far as we can go at the present time. I hope that you will all come back, so we can discuss the further development of the three stages of ati. That needs room and space. And at this point, we have been bombarded by all the yanas to the extent where we are uncertain who's who and what's what.

STUDENT: You mentioned that in the anuyoga yana, extremes could serve as a reference point for balance. Does this mean that there is still a reference point in the anuyoga yana?

TRUNGPA RINPOCHE: Yes, but it's a much better one. But we still haven't reached maha ati, so there's still a reference point. You see, finally, any technique, any method, any activity we might present becomes a reference point.

STUDENT: I still don't understand how the practice of mahamudra is integrated with visualization practice.

TRUNGPA RINPOCHE: The mahamudra practice is a highly visual thing. It is very much in tune with colors and sights and smells. It is so much in tune with any perceptions we might have, because there is no barrier anymore. So the visualization is not imagining something; you actually do feel whatever deity your practice is connected with. For instance, if you're doing a Kalachakra practice, you feel so overwhelmed by that that your life is completely bombarded by Kalachakra-ness.[3] Visualization comes to you and strikes you; therefore there's no problem with that. It's more a question of how far you're willing to go. It is a question of if you are willing to go too far or of the extent to which you are willing to go too far in opening, giving.

STUDENT: It seems to me that visualization would be an unnecessary side trip that could distract you from the essence of the mahamudra experience.

TRUNGPA RINPOCHE: That is possible. In fact the great Indian siddha Saraha attacked the idea of visualization, asking why there couldn't just be pure mahamudra without other trips. That is an expression of the mahamudra practice's yearning toward the maha ati level. It begins to break through, to become more revolutionary.

STUDENT: Could you explain how extreme compassion turns into extreme wrath?

TRUNGPA RINPOCHE: I don't know how to explain that. I mean, that's it. You have to experience it, I suppose. I could use all kinds of adjectives, but they would just be words.

STUDENT: What should you do upon meeting a wrathful deity?

TRUNGPA RINPOCHE: Meeting one? I don't think you meet them just like that. You become somewhat associated with that quality yourself. You are moving in that direction already, and so you're ready to see it, ready to experience that way.

S: So there would be some kind of identification with it?

TR: Yes, there would be some identification with it.

STUDENT: This extreme anger of the maha ati yanas—is that something that is directed toward the self and relates purely to one's own growth, or can this extreme anger with compassion manifest in the world?

TRUNGPA RINPOCHE: Manifest?

S: For someone who was at the level of the maha ati yanas, would this manifest in his teaching or purely in his practice, personally?

TR: I think it manifests in life experience altogether. There is a sense of crazy wisdom, of unreasonableness that is still being reasonable, a very dignified wildness that is very solid and very sharp at the same time. That manifests in relating to the lifestyles of individuals one is dealing with and in dealing with oneself.

There are all kinds of possibilities. Wherever there is energy, there is that possibility.

S: It's a kind of fervor that that kind of energy produces?

TR: It's a product of long experience of dismantling yourself, starting from the hinayana level.

STUDENT: Is there any relationship between the wrathful deities and vajra hell?

TRUNGPA RINPOCHE: Yes. That's the jail of the wrathful deities, I suppose you could say. And no one can save you from that.

S: So the wrathful deities put you in vajra hell and keep you there?

TR: No, not necessarily. The wrathful deities are by no means jail wardens. They are more like a powerful friend who does not go along with you if you do not go along with him.

STUDENT: Rinpoche, to what extent should these yanas and levels of awareness you're talking about be assimilated to Western forms, and to what extent to do you think they need to be kept in their traditional Tibetan form?

TRUNGPA RINPOCHE: I think people should have some understanding of the psychology of it, the whole idea of it, which is not a foreign idea, particularly. It's just general, universal logic, cosmic logic, that everybody could agree on. That is why the teaching is called the truth. Everybody can agree that fire is hot—it's that kind of thing. Once one has understood the basic principles of the tantric teaching and has had some experience of the practice of it, there should be no trouble in transplanting it. The images cease being seen as cultural expressions. They just become images on their own. So I think if people have a basic understanding of the psychology and philosophy, and especially if they have good background training in basic Buddhism—the hinayana and mahayana—tantra won't even need to be adopted. There's no need to try to cut it down or reduce it to make it presentable. If a person is able to feel it, see it, experience it, then it becomes almost too obvious. That's what seems to have happened in the past, in Tibet and also in Japan, when tantra was introduced. It was not adapted to anything. It was just transplanted—straight from the horse's mouth.

STUDENT: Is there a merging of the wrathful and peaceful deities? Or do you experience them one after the other?

TRUNGPA RINPOCHE: One after the other, yes. With either one of those, there's no choice. If there was a union, that would mean there would be some choice or compromise. But there's no compromise.

STUDENT: In the mahamudra yanas, visualization was important. When you get to maha ati, is visualization still necessary, or is there a more direct method?

TRUNGPA RINPOCHE: There is visualization up to a certain point. But it gets quite complicated here, because within maha ati itself, there are also three levels.

S: Well, let's say in the final stage of maha ati.

TR: No, there is no visualization.

S: But why is it necessary to have visualization to get to the great dzokpa chenpo?

TR: The basic purpose of visualization is to enable you to identify yourself with the principles of enlightenment and also to appreciate the colorfulness of the energy of the world around you at the same time. That way you can see your world as one of the deities. And, you know, it takes a lot of technique to enable you to do that, so that you begin to use head and heart together. Particularly the appreciation of energies in visual and auditory terms is very, very difficult. We probably feel that in listening to classical music or jazz, or some other kind of music, we are identifying with the sound, or going along with it or dancing with it; or when we watch a good movie, we might forget that we are sitting in a chair watching a movie. But in actual fact, we are fascinated rather than being one with the sound or the movie. So tuning in to the energy, cosmic energy, is very difficult. It's not a matter of just swinging with it. It needs a lot of techniques and manipulations, so to speak.

STUDENT: Rinpoche, is there an equivalent in Western psychology for anything approaching mahamudra? Like in Jung, perhaps?

TRUNGPA RINPOCHE: There is a touch of it in Jung, I suppose, but the problem is, it becomes so philosophical, rather than a matter of practice. It seems that he himself did not know how to handle the idea of practice. Anything on the mahamudra level could be a very profound and wild thing to talk about, but when it comes to how to practice it, people get very nervous—in case they might get sued.

STUDENT: How does one destroy power?

TRUNGPA RINPOCHE: By becoming completely one with the power. From the maha ati point of view.

STUDENT: Rinpoche, it's not clear to me how these eight logos are related to by the practitioner.

TRUNGPA RINPOCHE: I think it's very simple. Those practices are applicable if practitioners have difficulty relating with clarity or death or the proclamation of passion or the experience of penetration or the mother's curse. The whole thing is very practical. You might find to your surprise that you are challenged by all those elements already, but you are not conscious of those categories described in the texts.

S: Does the guru give the student practices that assist him in focusing on this or that particular matter? Does it go in a successive progression?

TR: It could go in progression or it could be training toward the development of your particular style as well.

S: So it must be very flexible.

TR: Yes, I think so. That's why, when you are working with tantric situations, you need a great deal of help from the guru, the benevolent dictator we discussed.

STUDENT: Is there any parallel between number eight, the spell of wrathful action, and the idea of the warrior? Especially in terms of challenge?

TRUNGPA RINPOCHE: I think so. If the warrior is training you in dealing with panic. Some people get completely paralyzed by a threat. They can't walk, they can't move, they become completely paralyzed. At that point the wise warrior would hit you very violently or decide to shoot you. Then you begin to pull yourself together by yourself and to carry out what you are doing properly. It is always possible that you might be too cowardly. You might see things so clearly that you become a coward. Then you have to be pushed, kicked, by the benevolent dictator.

STUDENT: Does the history of Tibet show that this complicated theology has been successful in bringing forth numbers of enlightened people?

TRUNGPA RINPOCHE: Yes. Right up to the present time. I experienced working with an enlightened teacher. There's no doubt about that. I'm a student of that enlightened person, and I am struggling as well to be a presumptuous person. So there's no doubt about that.

STUDENT: Are the eight logos cross-cultural? Is the reason they're unfamiliar to us that we are unfamiliar with those elements in ourselves or because we happen to be Americans?

TRUNGPA RINPOCHE: Tantra could be regarded as outlandish in any case. But it does have a transcultural element. It's like water. Anybody can drink water, including dogs and pigs.

The Italians and the Jews and the Americans can also drink water. It's a transpersonal substance.

STUDENT: When you were a student in Tibet, were you presented with this whole road map of the nine yanas before you started studying them?

TRUNGPA RINPOCHE: No, I wasn't. I was highly confused. I wish they had done this. That's why I'm doing it. I wanted to look at it myself and share it with the rest of the people. The training program we had in Tibet was unorganized and chaotic. It was extremely rich, but, you know, all over the place.

STUDENT: What is vajra hell like?

TRUNGPA RINPOCHE: It's pretty hellish, so hellish you can't even think of getting out of it. But when you do think of getting out of it, you are punished even more. If you develop any notion of duality, you are pulled back. If you develop even the notion of "me" existing, you will be pulled back, constantly sucked into the pain.

STUDENT: Could becoming Rudra be similar to being in vajra hell?

TRUNGPA RINPOCHE: Rudra is a candidate for vajra hell rather than a participant in it. Rudra has been enjoying himself too much, and he has to pay back for his enjoyment by going to vajra hell.

STUDENT: Is the candidate for vajra hell a person who has worked through all the yanas and then suddenly freaks out?

TRUNGPA RINPOCHE: I think until a person is caught up in the higher maha ati level of practice, he cannot be called a candidate for vajra hell. Up to the mahayana level, a person is immune to such consequences.

STUDENT: Are these herukas of the eight logos related to as yidams?

TRUNGPA RINPOCHE: Those are the yidams, yes. You could have one or another of them as a yidam.

STUDENT: These techniques that you've been describing in the tantric yanas sound so similar to brainwashing. Aside from the fact, which you made very clear, that we have to go through hinayana and mahayana to prepare the ground for tantra, is there really any difference between these techniques and other techniques?

TRUNGPA RINPOCHE: Definitely. These techniques are so daring, so personally challenging. Nothing else is that challenging. Other techniques provide confirmation, they create a nest, rather than exposing you to all kinds of cliffs where you could kill yourself or providing you with all kinds of instruments with which you could commit suicide. These techniques are so pointed, so crude and powerful, uncompassionate and wise, that you cannot really miss the point. Your fear is always there; that's the target they are getting to.

STUDENT: You spoke about the student developing a state of mind that was solid, direct, and unwavering. If that is the case, where do the mother's curse and vajra hell come into the picture?

TRUNGPA RINPOCHE: That's the whole point. As you get stronger and your state of mind gets more solid and unwavering, your strength has to be challenged. You can't just be born a solid person and go on solid without any reference point. So those provide the reference points or challenges. Until you get to maha ati, there are always challenges. There's always tickling and being pushed and pulled. That always happens.

STUDENT: To what extent do individuals have a choice not to do any of this? Are these challenges inevitable for everybody?

TRUNGPA RINPOCHE: Absolutely everybody. People are facing these things all the time in their everyday lives. But what we are doing is providing challenges that have a pattern and a workable orientation toward a path. That way the whole thing becomes more acute and precise.

I think we have to stop at this point. I would like to thank the audience for taking part in this. This seminar on the nine yanas has been one of the landmarks of my work in North America. I hope you will decide to stick with this, look through it some more, and study it. We could regard this particular situation, in May 1973 in San Francisco, as a historical occasion. True vajrayana and the true nine-yana principle have been introduced in America completely and thoroughly. I am glad there was no particular pride on the students' part, making a big point about having come here because of being confused or fucked up. The students here are serious in spite of some of them being dilettantes maybe. But at least you are serious dilettantes.

It is a very delightful thing that from today onward we will be approaching the point of working with American Buddhism in terms of the tantric teachings. You have taken part in the inauguration of it. Your being there made me say things, and I appreciate that very much. Your response has been fantastic, so kind and energetic at the same time. I am so pleased that you have witnessed this and participated in the bringing of tantra to America, properly, healthily, and officially—according to my boss. Thank you.

Notes

PART ONE

Chapter 1. The Journey

1. *Spiritual materialism* is a key term in the Vidyadhara's teaching. The first major book of his North American teachings was called *Cutting Through Spiritual Materialism* (Berkeley, Calif.: Shambhala Publications, 1973; reprinted 1987). Very simply, spiritual materialism means approaching spirituality with the intention of using it to achieve your preconceived ends rather than with an attitude of surrendering to reality.

Chapter 2. Hopelessness

1. The symbols for the twelve links (Skt. *nidana*) of the karmic chain of existence are a blind grandmother, the potter's wheel, a monkey, a person in a boat, a monkey in a six-windowed house, a married couple, an arrow through the eye, drinking milk and honey, gathering fruit, copulation, a woman in childbirth, a funeral procession.

2. The second and fourth of the great enlightened teachers of the Kagyü lineage of Tibetan Buddhism. Naropa (1016–1100) was one of the best known of the Indian *mahasiddhas,* or possessors of spiritual powers, as was his teacher Tilopa. Naropa's student Marpa (1012–1097) was a farmer and the first Tibetan lineage holder of the Kagyü lineage. His student Milarepa (1052–1135) is one of

Tibet's most famous saints, known for spending many years in retreat in remote mountain caves, then having many enlightened students. Milarepa's main student, Gampopa (1079–1153), founded the monastic order of the Kagyü.

3. Here and elsewhere in this book, Don Juan refers to the Yaqui Indian spiritual teacher depicted in the books of Carlos Castaneda.

4. Another way, besides the nine yanas, of delineating the Buddhist spiritual journey is in terms of the five paths. The five paths are the paths of accumulation, unification, seeing, meditation, and no more learning.

Chapter 3. The Preparation for Tantra

1. These two sentences ("First we prepare . . . Then we begin . . .") are a synopsis of the three main Buddhist yanas; hinayana, mahayana, and vajrayana.

2. The Vidyadhara is embarking on a description of five categories, sometimes known as the five powers (Skt. *bala*). The development of these five characterizes the path of unification. They are (with the Vidyadhara's eventual preferred English translations of them): faith (Skt. *shraddha;* Tib. *tepa*), exertion (Skt. *virya;* Tib. *tsöndrü*), mindfulness or recollection (Skt. *smriti;* Tib. *trenpa*), meditation (Skt. *dhyana;* Tib. *samten*), intellect (Skt. *prajna;* Tib. *sherap*). The fourth category is also often given as *samadhi* (Tib. *tingdzin*).

3. See *Shantideva* in Glossary.

4. According to the traditional cosmology of India, much of which became part of the Buddhist tradition, Mount Meru is the great cosmic mountain at the center of the universe.

5. The bodhisattva (Skt. "enlightenment being") is the ideal practitioner of the mahayana path. The bodhisattva's compassionate practice of virtues transcending ego is regarded as heroic and even warriorlike. The Vidyadhara discusses this in greater detail in part two, chapter 3, "The Dawn of Mysticism."

6. In Buddhism, the five skandhas (Tib. *phungpo,* meaning "heap" in both Sanskrit and Tibetan) are the five types of aggregates

of psychophysical factors that, taken together, are associated with the sense of self or ego. Upon examination, no such self or ego is found, only these collections. They are form (Skt. *rupa*), feeling (Skt. *vedana*), perception (Skt. *samjna*), formation (Skt. *samskara*), and conciousness (Skt. *vijnana*). See part two, chapter 2, "Competing with Our Projections."

7. *Chutzpa* (*ch* as in Scottish *Loch*) is a Yiddish word referring to boldness or audacity that proceeds vigorously rather than being cowed by obstacles.

Chapter 4. The Basic Body

1. The Vidyadhara describes the buddha families in more detail in part two, chapter 7, "The Five Buddha Families and Mahamudra." As stated, they are vajra, ratna, padma, karma, and buddha. Sometimes it is confusing when he refers to the last of these. Instead of spelling out the logically complete designation, "the buddha buddha family," he usually just calls it "the buddha family."

2. The five wisdoms are the enlightened expressions of the five buddha families. See part two, chapters 6, "Introduction to Tantra," and 7, "The Five Buddha Families and Mahamudra."

3. *Shunyata* (Skt. "emptiness") refers to the key mahayana notion that all dharmas (phenomena) are devoid of any autonomous essence. See part two, chapter 4, "The Juncture between Sutra and Tantra."

4. The Vidyadhara explains these points in the next chapter.

Chapter 5. The Crazy-Wisdom Holder and the Student

1. According to tradition, the Buddha, or enlightenment itself, has three modes of existence: dharmakaya, sambhogakaya, and nirmanakaya. These correspond to mind, speech, and body. The dharmakaya (Skt. "dharma body") is unoriginated, primordial mind, devoid of concept. The sambhogakaya ("enjoyment body") is its environment of compassion and communication. The nirmanakaya ("emanation body") is its physical form. The three kayas are also sometimes understood as existential levels, represented by buddhas. The dharmakaya buddha is supreme among these.

2. The Tibetan word *chö*, which literally means "cut off" or "cut through," designates a tantric practice the main part of which is cutting through the false concepts of ego by visualizing offering one's body to demons and requesting them to devour it.

Chapter 6. Alpha Pure

1. For more on vajra pride, see part two, chapter 6, "Introduction to Tantra."

2. *Satipatthana* is a Pali word (Skt. *smriti-upasthana*) meaning "four foundations of mindfulness." Working on the four foundations is one of the fundamental meditation practices of the hinayana. The four are mindfulness of body, mindfulness of life, mindfulness of effort, and mindfulness of mind. See Chögyam Trungpa, *The Heart of the Buddha* (Boston & London: Shambhala Publications, 1991), pp. 21–58.

3. See note 6 for chapter 6 on page 000.

PART TWO

Chapter 1. Suffering, Impermanence, Egolessness

1. These three qualities are traditionally referred to as the three marks of existence. They are most often listed as suffering, impermanence, and egolessness. The Vidyadhara refers to them again in the next chapter as pain, transitoriness, and nonsubstantiality.

Chapter 2. Competing with Our Projections

1. See note 6 for chapter 3 on page 214.

2. The Vidyadhara later decided in favor of "concept" as the best translation for the name of this fourth skandha. Some years later he revised his translation once more and ended up with "formation." He felt that "concept" was quite close to the actual process of the skandha, but "formation" was also excellent in this respect and closer to the Sanskrit *samskara*.

3. Paramita practices are discussed in the next chapter.

Chapter 3. The Dawn of Mysticism

1. Padmasambhava (fl. eighth century) was a great Indian teacher and saint, one of the founders of Buddhism in Tibet. For the Vidyadhara's account of this major figure, see Chögyam Trungpa, *Crazy Wisdom* (Boston & London: Shambhala Publications, 1991). For Milarepa, see Glossary.

2. One of the key doctrines in Buddhism concerns not falling into the two extremes of eternalism and nihilism. Eternalism is the hope or belief that something solid and permanent exists that guarantees salvation or at least some good result if we can connect with it, or various levels of failure if we cannot. Nihilism is the conviction that, since there are no solid or permanent reference points, and even cause and effect is meaningless, human effort is futile. *Madhyamaka,* which means "middle way" in Sanskrit, has the sense of a way between eternalism and nihilism, existence and nonexistence.

3. One of the landmarks of entering the mahayana is taking the bodhisattva vow to renounce one's own liberation from samsara in order to continue working for the liberation of all sentient beings.

4. *Paramita* is a Sanskrit word literally meaning "that which has reached the other shore."

5. It was not long after this that the Vidyadhara came up with the translation "exertion" for *virya,* with which he remained quite satisfied.

Chapter 4. The Juncture between Sutra and Tantra

1. The sutra teachings are those related to the first three yanas, which are sometimes referred to collectively as the *sutrayana* in counterdistinction to the six tantric yanas, which are sometimes known as the *tantrayana.* The sutra teachings are based on the class of scriptures of the same name, and the tantra teachings are based on the class of scriptures known as the tantras.

Chapter 5. Overcoming Moralism

1. *Bodhichitta* is a compound Sanskrit word. *Bodhi* means "awakened," and *chitta* means "mind." The term is often simply translated

"enlightenment" or the "mind of enlightenment." In spite of how it sounds, "transplantation of bodhichitta into one's mind" does not refer to bringing in a foreign element from outside. It means communicating the idea of enlightenment in such a way as to awaken the natural aspiration toward it that already exists within one.

2. These are meditative techniques used in the vajrayana, which Western students, in the period these talks were given, tended to seek out as picturesque and exotic esoterica. *Pranayama* refers to various kinds of special breathing techniques. Mudras here are various hand gestures that accompany liturgical practices, though the term has other meanings (cf. the discussions of mahamudra in the later talks). Visualization of deities is also dealt with in the later talks.

3. The following passage from Gampopa's *Jewel Ornament of Liberation,* translated by Herbert V. Guenther (Boston: Shambhala Publications, 1986), p. 208, might help to situate and clarify these remarks:

> The Vaibhāṣika declares: Atoms by nature are spherical, undivided, singular and exist physically. A mass of them is an object (of perception) such as colour-form and so on. When massed together, there are intervals between each one. They appear to be in one place, like a yak's tail [made up of many shifting hairs] in the pasture. They remain in a mass because they are held together by the Karma of sentient beings.
>
> The Sautrāntika claims that when atoms mass together there are no intervals between them, although they do not touch each other.
>
> Although these people make such statements, no proof is forthcoming. Atoms must be singular or plural. If singular they must have spatial divisions or not. If so they must have an eastern, western, southern, northern, upper and lower part. With these six parts their claim to singularity collapses. If they have no spatial divisions, all material things would have to

be of the nature of a single atom. But this clearly is not so. As is stated in the . . . 'Viṃśatikākarikā' (12):

> When one atom is joined with six others
> It follows that it must have six parts;
> If it is in the same place with six,
> The mass must be the same as one atom.

If you assume that there are many, there must have been one which by accumulation formed the mass. But since you cannot find a single atom physically, neither many atoms nor a single physical object having the nature of one can be found.

4. *The Heart Sutra* says: "Form is emptiness, emptiness is itself form; emptiness is no other than form, form is no other than emptiness."

5. Cf. note 2 for chapter 3, page 217.

6. Herbert V. Guenther (trans.), *The Life and Teaching of Naropa* (Boston & London: Shambhala Publications, 1986). Cf. also *Naropa* in Glossary.

7. See *Nagarjuna* in Glossary.

8. Herukas are male, and dakinis female, deities visualized in tantric practice as embodiments of various aspects of awakened mind. On *dharmakaya,* see note 1 for part one, chapter 5.

9. Guhyasamaja is one of the principal herukas of the anuttara yoga tantra.

Chapter 6. Introduction to Tantra

1. "Seed syllable" is *bija mantra* in Sanskrit: a single syllable, usually Sanskrit, that represents the essential reality of a particular deity.

2. The Nyingma is one of the four main orders of Buddhism in Tibet. It follows the earliest tradition of vajrayana Buddhism in Tibet, that of the Old Translation school. The other three orders are Kagyü, Sakya, and Gelug, which follow the New Translation school. See part two, chapter 9, "Mahamudra and Maha Ati."

3. See *Vajrasattva* in Glossary.

4. Atisha Dipankara (980/90–1055), a Buddhist scholar of royal family, was a teacher at the great Indian monastic university of Vikramashila. He spent the last twelve years of his life in Tibet and founded the Kadampa tradition of Tibetan Buddhism, which later merged with the Kagyü and Gelug traditions.

5. A person becoming a Buddhist takes refuge in the "three jewels," the Buddha, the dharma, and the sangha (the community of Buddhist practitioners). This means surrendering all other sources of refuge, such as prestige, wealth, or other doctrines.

6. Shamatha and vipashyana are the two main modes of meditation common to all forms of Buddhism. For shamatha (Tib. *shi-ne*), see part one, chapter 2, "Hopelessness." The Sanskrit term *vipashyana* (Pali *vipassana;* Tib. *lhakthong*) means "insight" or "clear seeing." Vipashyana meditation emphasizes broad or panoramic awareness rather than focused mindfulness as in shamatha. *Trenpa nyewar jokpa* is a Tibetan phrase that literally means "mindfulness or awareness that is resting closely." It refers to ongoing bare attention to every detail of the mind's activity through resting undistractedly in awareness. While this is, properly speaking, an aspect of shi-ne, it is also indispensable for the development of lhakthong.

7. See note 1 for chapter 5, on page 215.

Chapter 7. The Five Buddha Families and Mahamudra

1. This comment sounds a bit odd nowadays, but it accurately reflects tendencies of the early seventies, primarily associated with hippies but also cropping up in people of other sociological descriptions.

2. The jnana kaya is more usually referred to in this context as the *jnanasattva,* a Sanskrit term meaning "wisdom being." In the early tantric yanas, a distinction is made between the practitioner's visualization of the deity, which is known as the *samayasattva* (Skt. "commitment being"), and the jnanasattva. Whereas the samayasattva is regarded as the mere product of the practitioner's psychology,

the jnanasattva, which descends upon the samayasattva and empowers it, is considered to be the very reality of the deity.

3. Yogi Bhajan is a Sikh spiritual teacher who has a large following in America.

4. A yidam is a deity that a practitioner especially practices visualizing and identifying with, one that corresponds to his or her psychological makeup or basic nature.

Chapter 8. Anuttara Yoga

1. The word *vajra* has more than one meaning. Its principal sense is "indestructible" or "adamantine," as in the terms *vajrayana, vajra hell, vajra pride.* It is also used in this sense as an adjective in terms that are not fixed, such as here, in "vajra truth." Something is indestructible in this sense because it is self-existing; that is, it exists (and nonexists) beyond the play of duality. In the next talk, the Vidyadhara contrasts this sense of the word with the notion of "divine." In another sense that we encounter in this book, the term is applied as the name of one of the five buddha families.

2. *Samaya shila* is a Sanskrit term. *Samaya* refers to a sworn bond of mutual commitment between guru and disciple. The disciple is solemnly committed to the discipline (*shila*) of maintaining and further cultivating this bond with the guru, who represents the principle of totally awakened mind, or enlightenment.

3. Hevajra is one of the major heruka principles in the anuttara yoga tantra.

Chapter 9. Mahamudra and Maha Ati

1. According to the later tradition of Buddhism in Tibet, the tradition of the New Translation school, only four yanas make up the vajrayana. According to the older tradition, that of the Old Translation school, there are six yanas making up the vajrayana.

In the latter view, the anuttara yoga yana does not strictly count as a yana. The first three yanas are kriya yoga yana, upa yoga yana, and yoga yana. These are referred to as the lower tantras. The last three yanas are mahayoga yana, anuyoga yana, and atiyoga yana (or maha ati, as Vidyadhara Trungpa Rinpoche preferred to call it). These are referred to as the higher tantras.

Sometimes also, in the older tradition, these last three higher tantras are collectively called the anuttara yoga yana. This use of the same name does not, however, make the content of the higher tantras the same as that of the anuttara yoga yana according to the New Translation school. The anuttara yoga yana in the tradition of the New Translation school contains, among others, the great tantras of Kalachakra, Vajrayogini, Hevajra, Mahamaya, Chakrasamvara, Guhyasamaja. It is most especially these that the Vidyadhara has in mind when he associates the tantras of the New Translation school with mahamudra.

The Vidyadhara's exposition, although favoring the total of nine yanas and laying great weight on the final three, approaches a fusion of the older and later traditions.

2. For Naropa and Marpa, see Glossary. Virupa was one of the eighty-four Indian mahasiddhas, "great possessors of powers," famous for his miracles, including consuming immense quantities of wine.

3. Kalachakra (Skt. "wheel of time") is one of the main herukas of the anuttara yoga tantra.

Glossary

The definitions given in this glossary are particular to their usage in this book and should not be construed as the single or even most common meaning of a specific term. Unless designated otherwise, foreign terms in the glossary are Sanskrit.

abhisheka ("anointment") A ceremony in which a student is ritually introduced into a mandala of a particular tantric deity by a tantric master and is thus empowered to visualize and invoke that particular deity. The essential element of abhisheka is a meeting of minds between master and student.

amrita ("deathless") Consecrated liquor used in vajrayana meditation practices.

arhat A "worthy one," who has attained the highest level of hinayana.

bardo (Tib. "in-between state") A state between a previous state of experience and a subsequent one in which experience is not bound by either. There are six bardos, but the term is most commonly used to designate the state between death and rebirth.

bodhichitta "Awakened mind" or "enlightened mind."

bodhisattva   One who has committed himself or herself to the mahayana path of compassion and the practice of the six paramitas. The bodhisattva vow is one of relinquishing one's personal enlightenment to work for all sentient beings.

buddhadharma   The Buddha's teaching; Buddhism.

chakra   One of the primary centers of the illusory body. Most often, five are distinguished: head, throat, heart, navel, and secret centers.

chandali   A vajrayana term for a kind of psychic heat generated and experienced through certain meditative practices. This heat serves to burn up all types of obstacles and confusion.

dakini   A wrathful or semiwrathful female deity signifying compassion, emptiness, and transcendental knowledge. The dakinis are tricky and playful, representing the basic space of fertility out of which the play of samsara and nirvana arises. More generally, a dakini can be a type of messenger or protector.

dharma   The Buddha's teaching, or Buddhism; buddhadharma. Sometimes *dharma* is also used to mean "phenomenon."

dharmadhatu   The "space of things" or "space of phenomena." The all-encompassing, unoriginated, and unchanging space or totality of all phenomena.

dharmakaya   One of the three bodies of enlightenment. See note 1 for chapter 5 on page 215.

dharmata   The ultimate nature of reality; suchness.

dhyana   Meditation, one of the six paramitas.

duhkha   "Suffering." *Duhkha satya,* "the truth of suffering," is the first of Buddha's four noble truths. The term refers to physical and psychological suffering of all kinds, including the subtle but all-pervading frustration we experience with regard to the impermanence and insubstantiality of all things.

five buddha families   A tantric term referring to the mandala of the five sambhogakaya buddhas and the five fundamental principles of enlightenment they represent. In the mandala of enlightenment, these are five wisdom energies, but in the confused world of samsara, these energies arise as five confused emotions. Everything in the world is said to be predominantly characterized by one of these five. The following list gives the name of each family, its buddha, its wisdom, its confused emotion, and its direction and color in the mandala: (1) buddha, Vairochana, all-pervading wisdom, ignorance, center, white; (2) vajra, Akshobhya, mirrorlike wisdom, aggression, east, blue; (3) ratna (jewel), Ratnasambhava, wisdom of equanimity, pride, south, yellow; (4) padma (lotus), Amitabha, discriminating-awareness wisdom, passion, west, red; (5) karma (action), Amoghasiddhi, all-accomplishing wisdom, north, green. Some of these qualities differ slightly in different tantras.

four noble truths   The basis of the Buddhist teaching. The four noble truths are (1) the truth of suffering, (2) the truth of the origin of suffering, (3) the truth of the cessation of suffering, (4) the truth of the path that leads to the cessation of suffering.

heruka   A wrathful male deity.

hinayana   The "lesser" vehicle, in which the practitioner concentrates on basic meditation practice and an understanding of basic Buddhist doctrines such as the four noble truths.

jnana   The wisdom-activity of enlightenment, transcending all dualistic conceptualization.

karma   Literally, "action." In a general sense, the law of cause and effect: positive actions bring happiness; negative actions bring suffering.

kilaya   A three-edged ritual dagger.

mahamudra   The "great seal," one of the highest teachings in the vajrayana. See part one, chapter 4, "The Basic Body," and part two, chapter 7, "The Five Buddha Families and Mahamudra."

mahayana The "great vehicle," which emphasizes the emptiness (shunyata) of all phenomena, compassion, and the acknowledgment of universal buddha nature. The ideal figure of the mahayana is the bodhisattva; hence it is often referred to as the bodhisattva path.

mandala A total vision that unifies the seeming complexity and chaos of experience into a simple pattern and natural hierarchy. The Tibetan word *khyilkhor* used to translate the Sanskrit term literally means "center and surroundings." A mandala is usually represented two-dimensionally as a four-sided diagram with a central deity, a personification of the basic sanity of buddha nature. Three-dimensionally, it is a palace with a center and four gates in the cardinal directions.

mantra A combination of words (usually Sanskrit) or syllables that expresses the quintessence of a tantric deity. A mantra may or may not have conceptual content. Recitation of mantra is a vajrayana practice that is always done in conjunction with visualization.

Marpa (1012–1097) Marpa Lotsawa (Marpa the Translator), was the third of the great enlightened teachers of the Kagyü lineage of Tibet and the first Tibetan of that lineage. He was an unruly farmer's son who made three epic journeys to India in search of the dharma. There he became the student of Naropa and other gurus, which enabled him to bring the tantric Buddhist teachings back to Tibet. His most famous student was Milarepa. See *The Life of Marpa the Translator,* translated by the Nālandā Translation Committee under the direction of Chögyam Trungpa (Boston & London: Shambhala Publications, 1986).

Milarepa (1052–1135) "Mila the Cotton-Clad" was the fourth great enlightened teacher in the Kagyü lineage of Tibetan Buddhism. A black magician in his youth, he underwent a period of extreme hardship and trial at the hands of his guru Marpa. He then spent many years in solitary meditation in caves in the high mountains of Tibet before attaining enlightenment and attracting many students. His chief student was Gampopa (1079–1153). See Lobsang P. Lhalungpa (trans.), *The Life of Milarepa* (Boston & London: Shambhala Publications, 1985).

mudra   Most often the term is used to refer to symbolic hand gestures that accompany the vajrayana practices of visualization and mantra recitation. More generally, *mudra* refers to the provocative highlights of phenomena.

Nagarjuna (second/third century)   was a great Indian teacher of Buddhism, the founder of the Madhyamaka school of Buddhist philosophy. He contributed greatly to the logical development of the doctrine of shunyata and was the author of many key texts as well as, in legend, the guru of various important Buddhist teachers who lived centuries apart.

Naropa (1016–1100)   was a great Indian siddha, second of the great enlightened teachers of the Kagyü lineage of Tibetan Buddhism. See Herbert V. Guenther (trans.), *The Life and Teaching of Naropa* (Boston & London: Shambhala Publications, 1986).

nidanas   The twelve "links" of the karmic chain of existence. See note 1 for chapter 2 on page 213.

nirvana   The idea of enlightenment according to the hinayana. It is the cessation of ignorance and conflicting emotions and therefore freedom from compulsive rebirth in samsara.

Padmasambhava   Padmasambhava, also referred to as Guru Rinpoche, or "Precious Teacher," introduced vajrayana Buddhism to Tibet in the eighth century. (See note 1 for chapter 3, pages 216–17.)

paramita   ("that which has reached the other shore")   The six paramitas, or "perfections," are generosity, discipline, patience, exertion, meditation, and knowledge.

prajna   Literally, "transcendental knowledge." Prajna, the sixth paramita, is called transcendental because it sees through the veils of dualistic confusion.

pratyekabuddha   One who concentrates on his or her own liberation without being concerned about helping others. The pratyekabuddha's approach characterizes the second of the nine yanas.

preta   A hungry ghost, one of the six kinds of beings in the samsaric realms. The other five are gods, jealous gods, humans, animals, and hell beings.

Rudra   Originally a Hindu deity, an emanation of Shiva. In the vajrayana, Rudra is the personification of the destructive principle of ultimate ego. According to tradition, Rudra was originally a tantric student who perverted the teachings and killed his guru. He was thus transformed into Rudra, the embodiment of egohood, the complete opposite of buddhahood.

samaya   The vajrayana principle of commitment, whereby the student's total experience is bound to the path.

sambhogakaya   One of the three bodies of enlightenment. See note 1 for chapter 5 on page 215.

samsara   The vicious cycle of transmigratory existence. It arises out of ignorance and is characterized by suffering.

sangha   The community of people devoted to the three jewels of Buddha, dharma, and sangha: the Buddha, his teaching, and this community itself. The term preeminently refers to the Buddhist monastic community.

shamatha   A basic meditation practice common to most schools of Buddhism, the aim of which is developing tranquillity through mindfulness.

Shantideva   A prince (fl. seventh/eighth century C.E.) who became a Buddhist monk and a teacher of the Madhyamaka school of mahayana Buddhism. He was the author of the *Bodhicharyavatara,* a classic text of the mahayana, written in a beautiful poetic style. One English translation is *Entering the Path of Enlightenment,* translated by M. L. Matics (New York: Macmillan Company, 1970). Another is *A Guide to the Bodhisattva's Way of Life* (Dharamsala, India: Library of Tibetan Works and Archives, 1979).

shila   Discipline, the second paramita.

shravaka   Shravaka was a disciple who actually heard the teachings of the Buddha directly. With a small *s*, the term is also the name of the first of the nine yanas, in which the practitioner concentrates on basic meditation practice and an understanding of basic Buddhist doctrines such as the four noble truths.

shunyata   ("emptiness")   A completely open and unbounded clarity of mind.

siddha   One who possesses siddhis, or "perfect abilities." There are eight ordinary siddhis: indomitability, the ability to see the gods, fleetness of foot, invisibility, longevity, the ability to fly, the ability to make certain medicines, and power over the world of spirits and demons. The single "supreme" siddhi is enlightenment.

skandha   ("heap")   One of the five types of aggregates of psychophysical factors that are associated with the sense of self or ego. See note 6 for chapter 3 on page 214.

sutra   One of the hinayana and mahayana texts that are attributed to Shakyamuni Buddha. A sutra is usually a dialogue between the Buddha and one or more of his disciples, elaborating on a particular topic of dharma.

tantra   A synonym for *vajrayana*, the third of the three main yanas of the buddhadharma. The vajrayana teachings are said to have been taught by the Buddha in his sambhogakaya form. They are recorded in scriptures known as tantras. *See also* vajrayana.

tathagatagarbha   A term of primary importance for the mahayana. *Tathagatha* literally means "thus-gone" and is an epithet for a fully realized buddha. *Garbha* means "embryo" or "egg."

The term refers to buddha nature, the enlightened basic nature of all beings, which the mahayana regards as being temporarily covered over by dualistic confusions. It is compared to the sun behind clouds or a jewel in a dung heap.

three marks of existence A basic Buddhist doctrine. Existence is characterized by suffering, impermanence, and egolessness. See part two, chapter 1, "Suffering, Impermanence, Egolessness."

The Tibetan Book of the Dead (Tib. *Bardo Thödol,* "Book of Liberation in the Bardo through Hearing") This famous text sets forth the process of death and rebirth and how to become liberated from it. Its origin can be traced to Padmasambhava.

vajra A vajra is a tantric ritual implement or scepter representing a thunderbolt, the scepter of the king of the gods, Indra. This thunderbolt is said to be made of adamantine or diamond, and this is connected with its basic symbolism: the indestructibility of awakened mind. When used with the ritual bell, or *ghanta,* the vajra symbolizes skillful means, and the bell, transcendental knowledge. Vajra is also the name of one of the five buddha families, whose enlightened quality is pristine clarity and whose confused or neurotic quality is aggression.

Vajrasattva One of the deities visualized at various levels of tantric practice. He is associated with primordial purity.

vajrayana ("diamond vehicle") The third of the three main yanas of the buddhadharma, synonymous with *tantra.* It is divided into six, or sometimes four, subsidiary vehicles.

vidyadhara "Knowledge-holder," "crazy-wisdom holder."

vipashyana "Insight" or "clear seeing." With shamatha, one of the two main modes of meditation common to all forms of Buddhism. See note 6 for chapter 6 on page 220.

virya Exertion, one of the six paramitas.

yana ("vehicle") A coherent body of intellectual teachings and practical meditative methods related to a particular stage of a student's progress on the path of buddhadharma. The three main vehicles are the hinayana, mahayana, and vajrayana. These can also be subdivided to make nine yanas.

yidam The vajrayana practitioner's personal deity, who embodies the practitioner's awakened nature. Yidams are usually sambho-gakaya buddhas.

Transliterations of Tibetan Terms

Chemchok	*che mchog*
chö	*gcod*
dzokpa chenpo	*rdzogs pa chen po*
Jikten Chötö	*'jig rten mchod bstod*
ka	*bka'*
kadak	*ka dag*
khorde yerme	*'khor 'das dbyer med*
la-me	*bla med*
lhakthong	*lhag mthong*
lhayi ngagyal	*lha yi nga rgyal*
Mamo Bötong	*ma mo rbod gtong*
Möpa Trag-ngak	*dmod pa drag sngags*
nyam kongphel	*nyams gong 'phel*
rikpa tsephep	*rig pa tshad phebs*
samten	*bsam gtan*
sherap	*shes rap*
shi	*gzhi*
shi-ne	*gzhi gnas*
tampe tön ni jikpa me	*dam pa'i don ni 'jigs pa med*
tamtsik	*dam tshig*

tepa	*dad pa*
tingdzin	*ting 'dzin*
trenpa	*dran pa*
trenpa nyewar jokpa	*dran pa nye bar 'jog pa*
tsöndrü	*brtson 'grus*
Yangdak	*yang dag*
yeshe chölwa	*ye shes 'chol ba*
yidam	*yi dam*

About the Author

Ven. Chögyam Trungpa was born in the province of Kham in Eastern Tibet in 1940. When he was just thirteen months old, Chögyam Trungpa was recognized as a major *tülku,* or incarnate teacher. According to Tibetan tradition, an enlightened teacher is capable, based on his or her vow of compassion, of reincarnating in human form over a succession of generations. Before dying, such a teacher leaves a letter or other clues to the whereabouts of the next incarnation. Later, students and other realized teachers look through these clues and, based on careful examination of dreams and visions, conduct searches to discover and recognize the successor. Thus, particular lines of teaching are formed, in some cases extending over several centuries. Chögyam Trungpa was the eleventh in the teaching lineage known as the Trungpa Tülkus.

Once young tülkus are recognized, they enter a period of intensive training in the theory and practice of the Buddhist teachings. Trungpa Rinpoche (*Rinpoche* is an honorific title meaning "precious one"), after being enthroned as supreme abbot of Surmang Monasteries and governor of Surmang District, began a period of training that would last eighteen years, until his departure from Tibet in 1959. As a Kagyü tülku, his training was based on the systematic practice of meditation and on refined theoretical understanding of Buddhist philosophy. One of the four great lineages of Tibet, the Kagyü is know as the "practice lineage."

At the age of eight, Trungpa Rinpoche received ordination as a novice monk. After his ordination, he engaged in intensive study and practice of the traditional monastic disciplines as well as in the arts of calligraphy, thangka painting, and monastic dance. His primary teachers were Jamgön Kongtrül of Sechen and Khenpo Kangshar—leading teachers in the Nyingma and Kagyü lineages. In 1958, at the age of eighteen, Trungpa Rinpoche completed his studies, receiving the degrees of *kyorpön* (doctor of divinity) and *khenpo* (master of studies). He also received full monastic ordination.

The late fifties were a time of great upheaval in Tibet. As it became clear that the Chinese Communists intended to take over the country by force, many people, both monastic and lay, fled the country. Trungpa Rinpoche spent many harrowing months trekking over the Himalayas (described in his book *Born in Tibet*). After narrowly escaping capture by the Chinese, he at last reached India in 1959. While in India, Trungpa Rinpoche was appointed by His Holiness Tenzin Gyatso, the fourteenth Dalai Lama, to serve as spiritual advisor to the Young Lamas Home School in Dalhousie, India. He served in this capacity from 1959 to 1963.

Trungpa Rinpoche's first opportunity to encounter the West came when he received a Spaulding sponsorship to attend Oxford University. At Oxford he studied comparative religion, philosophy, and fine arts. He also studied Japanese flower arranging, receiving a degree from the Sogetsu School. While in England, Trungpa Rinpoche began to instruct Western students in the dharma (the teachings of the Buddha), and in 1968 he founded the Samye Ling Meditation Centre in Dumfriesshire, Scotland. During this period he also published his first two books, both in English: *Born in Tibet* and *Meditation in Action*.

In 1969, Trungpa Rinpoche traveled to Bhutan, where he entered into a solitary meditation retreat. This retreat marked a pivotal change in his approach to teaching. Immediately upon returning he became a lay person, putting aside his monastic robes and dressing in ordinary Western attire. He also married a young Englishwoman, and together they left Scotland and moved to North America. Many of his early students found these changes shocking and upsetting. However, he expressed a conviction that, in order to take root in the West, the dharma needed to be taught free from cultural trappings and religious fascination.

During the seventies America was in a period of political and cultural ferment. It was a time of fascination with the East. Trungpa Rinpoche criticized the materialistic and commercialized approach to spirituality he encountered, describing it as a "spiritual supermarket." In his lectures, and in his books *Cutting Through Spiritual Materialism* and *The Myth of Freedom,* he pointed to the simplicity and directness of the practice of sitting meditation as the way to cut through such distortions of the spiritual journey.

During his seventeen years of teaching in North America, Trungpa Rinpoche developed a reputation as a dynamic and controversial teacher. Fluent in the English language, he was one of the first lamas who could speak to Western students directly, without the aid of a translator. Traveling extensively throughout North America and Europe, Trungpa Rinpoche gave hundreds of talks and seminars. He established major centers in Vermont, Colorado, and Nova Scotia, as well as many smaller meditation and study centers in cities throughout North America and Europe. Vajradhatu was formed in 1973 as the central administrative body of this network.

In 1974, Trungpa Rinpoche founded the Naropa Institute, which became the only accredited Buddhist-inspired university in North America. He lectured extensively at the Institute, and his book *Journey without Goal* is based on a course he taught there. In 1976, he established the Shambhala Training program, a series of weekend programs and seminars that provides instruction in meditation practice within a secular setting. His book *Shambhala: The Sacred Path of the Warrior* gives an overview of the Shambhala teachings.

In 1976, Trungpa Rinpoche appointed Ösel Tendzin (Thomas F. Rich) as his Vajra Regent, or dharma heir. Ösel Tendzin worked closely with Trungpa Rinpoche in the administration of Vajra-dhatu and Shambhala Training. He taught extensively from 1976 until his death in 1990 and is the author of *Buddha in the Palm of Your Hand*.

Trungpa Rinpoche was also active in the field of translation. Working with Francesca Fremantle, he rendered a new translation of *The Tibetan Book of the Dead*, which was published in 1975. Later he formed the Nālandā Translation Committee, in order to translate texts and liturgies for his own students as well as to make important texts available publicly.

In 1978 Trungpa Rinpoche conducted a ceremony empowering his son Ösel Rangdröl Mukpo as his successor in the Shambhala lineage. At that time he gave him the title of Sawang, or "earth lord."

Trungpa Rinpoche was also known for his interest in the arts and particularly for his insights into the relationship between contemplative discipline and the artistic process. His own art work included calligraphy, painting, flower arranging, poetry, play-writing, and environmental installations. In addition, at the Naropa Institute he created an educational atmosphere that attracted many leading artists and poets. The exploration of the creative process in light of contemplative training continues there as a provocative dialogue. Trungpa Rinpoche also published two books of poetry: *Mudra* and *First Thought Best Thought*.

Trungpa Rinpoche's published books represent only a fraction of the rich legacy of his teachings. During his seventeen years of teaching in North America, he crafted the structures necessary to provide his students with thorough, systematic training in the dharma. From introductory talks and courses to advanced group retreat practices, these programs emphasize a balance of study and practice, of intellect and intuition. Students at all levels can pursue their interest in meditation and the Buddhist path through these many forms of training. Senior students of Trungpa Rinpoche continue to be involved in both teaching and meditation instruction in such programs. In addition to his extensive teachings in the Buddhist tradition, Trungpa Rinpoche also placed great emphasis on the Shambhala teachings, which stress the importance of mind-training, as distinct from religious practice; community involvement and the creation of an enlightened society; and appreciation of one's day-to-day life.

Trungpa Rinpoche passed away in 1987, at the age of forty-seven. He is survived by his wife, Diana, and five sons. His eldest son, the Sawang Ösel Rangdröl Mukpo, succeeds him as president and spiritual head of Vajradhatu. By the time of his death, Trungpa Rinpoche had become known as a pivotal figure in introducing dharma to the Western world. The joining of his great appreciation for Western culture and his deep understanding of his own tradition led to a revolutionary approach to teaching the dharma, in which the most ancient and profound teachings were presented in a thoroughly contemporary way. Trungpa Rinpoche was known for his fearless proclamation of the dharma: free from hesitation, true to the purity of the tradition, and utterly fresh. May these teachings take root and flourish for the benefit of all sentient beings.

Meditation Center Information

For further information regarding meditation or inquiries about a dharma center near you, please contact one of the following centers.

Karme-Chöling
Star Route
Barnet, VT 05821
(802) 633-2384

Rocky Mountain Dharma Center
4921 County Road 68C
Red Feather Lakes, CO 80545
(303) 881-2184

Vajradhatu Europe
Zwetchenweg 23
D3550 Marburg
Germany
49 6421 34244

Vajradhatu International
1084 Tower Road
Halifax, N.S. B3H 2Y5
Canada
(902) 425-4275

Many talks and seminars are available in cassette tape format. For information, call or write:

Vajradhatu Recordings
1084 Tower Road
Halifax, N.S. B3H 2Y5
(902) 421-1550

Index